Invisible England

The Testimony of David Hanson

Anya Chaika

Chalk Circle Press

To Dave and Becky

THE JUDGE: Officer, fetch a piece of chalk. You will trace below the bench a circle, in the centre of which you will place the child. Then you will order the two women to wait, each of them at the opposite sides of the circle, but the pretended mother cannot lead him out. *(The OFFICER traces a circle with the chalk and motions the child to stand in the centre of it. MRS MA takes the child's hand and leads him out of the circle. HAI-TANG fails to contend with her.)*

THE JUDGE: It is evident that Hai-Tang is not the mother of the child, since she did not come forward to draw him out of the circle.

HAI-TANG: I supplicate you, Honoured Sir, to calm your wrath. If I cannot obtain my son without dislocationg his arm or dislocating his baby flesh, I would rather perish under the blows than make the least effort to take him out of the circle.

THE JUDGE: A sage of old once said: What man can hide who he really is? Behold the power of the Chalk Circle! In order to seize an inheritance, Mrs Ma has raised a child that is not her own. But the chalk circle augustly brought out the truth and the falsehood. Mrs Ma has an engaging exterior but her heart is corrupt. The true mother – Hai-Tang – is at last recognised.

From *The Chalk Circle*, an anonymous Chinese play of about 1300 A.D.

Contents

Prologue

There were many occasions when I met David for the first time. I met him right at the beginning when I discovered his deleted blog in an obscure part of the internet; I met him again on Facebook when he was looking for other survivors and, finally, I met him when he picked me up in his battered Peugeot at Taunton train station on the way to see his solicitor. Each time I met him he was exactly as I thought he would be. That jolt of surprise when you first meet someone in the flesh after a long relationship never came. He was awkward, straightforward, prickly, charming, frustrating and genuine on every occasion we spoke.

I have often wondered what it is about David that has allowed him to survive and keep himself together enough to tell his story. There are probably a million reasons why he is the person he became but there are some things which seem to stand out. First, he appears to have that ability to hold what is most true to him deep inside himself and to bring it out in the open when he needs to develop and nuture it. He met his long-term partner, and mother of his two children, at a young age and she seems to have been a constant source of support for him. The relationship has probably acted as a clear and undistorted mirror in which he has been able to see the terrifying events which surrounded him. He also has his music. In his car, on our way to filming our first interview with him, he put on a tape of his cover versions of country and western music. I asked if we could listen to his original work and he refused, saying he only ever played it to his partner.

Although this is his story, in some ways he is telling it for all the others. There is little doubt that there are thousands of children who have experienced this treatment in the USA, Germany, the Czech Republic, Australia and other countries. It is hoped that this account will enable these other children to speak about what was done to them and that these accounts will prevent these practices ever taking place again.

The Beginning

But your spine has been smashed,
My beautiful, pitiful era,
And an inane smile
You look back cruel and weak
Like an animal past its prime
At the prints of its own paws

Osip Mandalstam, "Vek"

It all began for me when I returned to England after having lived for many years in Moscow. I had been working for the British Council as a teacher and my wife had worked first for Boris Berezovsky, the billionaire oligarch, and then, later, for a children's rights charity. The city itself was still traumatised by the fall of the Soviet Union, when society seemed to have collapsed in on itself and devastated the lives of millions. My local train station was full of refugees from rural children's homes who slept on underground hot water pipes to keep warm and who were then rounded up by the police and dumped in a distant field whenever a local dignitary came into town. Not all of them made it back to the station.

When I first arrived it was just after the August coup in 1991 and the whole city was still grey and depressed. We lived in a flat on Spiridonovka Street, about 15 minutes' walk from the Kremlin, and the heavy winter coats we all wore seemed to protect us from the oppression just as much as from the cold. My wife and I spent our days walking around Patriarchy Ponds and, later on in the summer, meeting our friends in the cafes and restaurants that had begun to spring up around the city.

At first, we lived with my parents-in-law and I learnt what it must have been like to live in a *Kommunalka*, the large nineteenth century flats where each ornate room was occupied by a whole family. It was easier for us though because my wife's parents were so quiet, especially her father, Volodya. I asked about this and she told me a story about his childhood. As a boy he had lived in the same flat as his parents and grandparents. His grandfather was a big cheese in the Communist Party and a measure of this was that he was allowed to travel abroad, almost unheard of for the ordinary man. He went to America during the cold war and was famous for bringing back the secret for making choc-ices – apparently getting the thin chocolate coat on the ice-cream was a real breakthrough. Later on, he fell from favour and very late one night the KGB knocked on their door and took him away to the Gulag. Such was the fear that nobody in the family mentioned it for 20 years. They knew that they couldn't trust anyone completely, even family members. Volodya was eight then. "He didn't talk much after that", said my mother-in-law.

When my wife and I lived in the flat by ourselves we had many visitors. Our friends were the sons and daughters of Soviet artists and they themselves later became fashion designers, painters and film-makers in the new Russia. Just then, when they were still in their teens, they huddled together in their group, enjoying the genuine art that had been lovingly passed on from their parents and which helped them survive the terrible changes that were going on around them.

Throughout the 1990s I lived with my wife and our young son in the city during the week and, at the weekend, we travelled to the countryside. The family country house, originally a large wooden building in the middle of a garden, had been divided up into tiny sections and so most of our days there were spent outside – going for walks and watching huge, garish homes being built for the new super-rich.

My work as a teacher for the British Council took me to Yakusk in the Russian Far East, Vladivostok and the former Soviet republics of Estonia and Uzbeckistan. I worked like this for six years until the politicians got involved and the whole project was closed down. It was the end of the revolution in Russia and the start of another. Seventy years of oppression were slowly being dismantled and, before any good could come from it the suffering had to take place. The average age of an adult male dropped to 50, corruption touched every part of society and crime rocketed. Yet, in spite of the chaos, new institutions were created, people travelled abroad for the first time and a new openness had started to moderate the old ways of doing things.

When I returned to England I was grateful for the lack of corruption and the way you could just walk down the street and not have to pay a bribe to a policeman just because you didn't have your passport. I worked mainly as a children's social worker and I had a caseload of children who were either in care or on the Child Protection Register. In 2009, after working in a number of local authorities, I started work for a children's advocacy charity and it was here that I first came across the practices that made me wonder whether I had fallen asleep and woken up in a novel.

We had many local authority contracts and a few private ones. If a child was in care and needed someone to give them a voice we would provide an advocate and legal advice. We also helped them with formal complaints and went to meetings with them. The thing that we did best was to quote from them directly in our reports and records. If children said something we put it in context but we would put it down word for word or give them a pen, or even drawing materials to help them tell it the way they wanted. A good advocate could do a great deal to change a child's life.

One of the private contracts I was responsible for was a group of 11 children's residential homes, which were known as K. homes. We provided advocates who would, every month, visit the homes and talk to the children as a group. I managed this contract for nine months without the slightest idea that there was anything out of the ordinary about it. Looking back on it there was something odd about the set-up. It was true that the monthly reports would come through on my computer for each home and that there was a stream of information recording when the advocate had visited, which children were present, that the food was boring or that somebody was being bullied and didn't feel that it was being sorted out. This in itself was perfectly usual but, as the invoices were sent out, they were paid immediately and there was no questioning of the figures, or indeed questioning of any kind. Every other client would demand meetings and breakdowns of the statistics. From this contract we heard nothing.

The phone call came out of the blue. My manager had said nothing to indicate there was anything unusual going on and supervision consisted simply of discussions about invoices and the difficulties I was having in getting to see J., the group manager. Over time this difficulty had become increasingly frustrating and the most recent excuse was that J. had apparently broken her leg and would be in touch. In August I tried to call one last time and, to my surprise, was put through. "I suppose we had better meet up," she said reluctantly. So we arranged a time and, just as she was about to hang up, she added, "One of your advocates has been complaining."

Looking back, it was probably this phrase that marked the beginning of it all. The moment when a hidden world started to open up and I began to learn of things that I had no idea existed

"She doesn't like what we do, you know", she said. "She caused a lot of trouble when she spoke to a social worker about the therapy."

"What doesn't she like?"

"She just doesn't like the therapy. I told her that if she's got a problem she needs to come to us, not to the social worker"

I finished the call and phoned the advocate. "What's this all about?" I asked. She started talking about the every-day troubles you get in any contract. I asked her specifically about the treatment and it was then that she used the term "holding therapy". This was the first time I had heard the words that I would hear many times again in the future.

"I don't agree with it," she said. "I've spoken to a friend about it, a therapist - she doesn't like it either." I tried to get some more detail and she spoke at length but meandered around without ever really getting back to the point she had been making.

After I put the phone down I stared out of the floor-to-ceiling windows that lined my side of the office. The rain blurred the view of the nineteenth century docks that I looked out on every day and I noticed for the first time the little pencil drawings that were made on post-it notes stuck to the window frames - my predecessor had, every now and again, recorded the comings and goings of boats, birds and passersby. The squares of paper were now little snapshots of moments in time which nobody else had noticed.

At the next desk sat the head of training, a clear-eyed and experienced professional who travelled the country training advocates. "I've just had a bizarre phone call about therapy at the K programme. Do you know anything about this?"

"I just know it's called holding therapy...really controversial apparently." She paused for thought for a few seconds. "I saw this documentary once," she said. "It was all about this kid who was being held down by his parents and the therapists. He just kept on saying, "'Get off me! Get off me!'" I just thought, you know, what the hell is going on?"

I rang a second advocate, someone who had been visiting the K. homes for years. He was well respected as a social worker, and as a advocate, and I was sure he could get to the point. "Glad you asked me that," he said when I rang him. "I've had concerns for some time." I was relieved. "Thank God," I thought, "I'm finally going to find out what's going on." But then, like the first advocate, he started talking about the same problems that you get in any residential home full of vulnerable children and underpaid staff. "Hang on, what about the therapy?" I asked. He went quiet for a moment and said, "I know it's intrusive but that's all I know."

"What, after 10 years that's all you know?"

He paused again and then said, "It's like a cult.". He said the word quietly but in a very clipped way, almost as an expression of self-disgust. "Everyone in the organisation has been made to think this way and nobody can question anything. It's injected into them." The words tumbled out of him and I could tell that he wanted to put them back in almost as much as he wanted them to come out. He qualified himself after this but the things he had said had been buried for some time and there was no doubting their spontaneity. I hung up the phone and rang the third and fourth advocates. They said they knew little of the therapy and presumed it involved talking. "So you never spoke about the therapy with the young people over the years? You never asked them where they were going every week? Weren't you curious?" I thought at the time that they were being dishonest but I have since come to an understanding that some people have a remarkable capacity for avoiding uncomfortable truths.

Looking back, I am amazed that I managed to work as a children's social worker for eight years without ever coming across holding therapy. These eight years included work in many different councils, with large numbers of lawyers, psychiatrists, psychologists, therapists, residential workers and foster carers. I could understand that a member of the public might not be aware but how could professionals in the field be so ignorant of this?

It was then that I started to research the subject. There were a number of articles in American peer-reviewed psychology journals, an organisation called Advocates for Children in Therapy (ACT) and some specially commissioned reports. Wikipedia provided me with a surprisingly detailed account of the background and the entry on holding therapy, was mainly written by a professor of child psychology. It describes how holding therapy, also known as attachment therapy, was developed in the 1970s in the USA and was widely used in clinics in the Evergreen, Colorado from the 1980s onwards.

The entry discussed the origins of the practice and the

theoretical background but what I really needed to know was what actually happened in the therapy sessions. Further down in the entry I found what I was looking for, a description of the use of holding therapy in a US clinic:

> The Center induces rage by physically restraining the child and forcing eye contact with the therapist (the child must lie across the laps of two therapists, looking up at one of them). In a workshop handout prepared by two therapists at The Center, the following sequence of events is described: (1) therapist "forces control" by holding (which produces child "rage"); (2) rage leads to child "capitulation" to the therapist, as indicated by the child breaking down emotionally ("sobbing"); (3) the therapist takes advantage of the child's capitulation by showing nurturance and warmth; (4) this new trust allows the child to accept "control" by the therapist and eventually the parent. According to The Center's treatment protocol, if the child "shuts down" (*i.e.*, refuses to comply), he or she may be threatened with detainment for the day at the clinic or forced placement in a temporary foster home; this is explained to the child as a consequence of not choosing to be a "family boy or girl." If the child is actually placed in foster care, the child is then required to "earn the way back to therapy" and a chance to resume living with the adoptive family.[14]

This was difficult to take in. Wasn't therapy with vulnerable children meant to take great care with children's emotions? Surely you can't force children to love someone. Didn't this go against everything that was contained in attachment

14

theory? I struggled to understand this and relate it to my experiences of working in children's social work

The entry went on to quote the American Professional Society on the Abuse of Children (APSAC):

> A central feature of many of these therapies is the use of psychological, physical, or aggressive means to provoke the child to catharsis, ventilation of rage, or other sorts of acute emotional discharge. To do this, a variety of coercive techniques are used, including scheduled holding, binding, rib cage stimulation (e.g., tickling, pinching, knuckling), and/or licking. Children may be held down, may have several adults lie on top of them, or their faces may be held so they can be forced to engage in prolonged eye contact. Sessions may last from 3 to 5 hours, with some sessions reportedly lasting longer... Similar but less physically coercive approaches may involve holding the child and psychologically encouraging the child to vent anger toward her or his biological parent.[2]

Looking back, I remember feeling a real sense of horror and disbelief as my mind started to process this. This kind of thing couldn't be happening in England. I thought about the commonplace way the advocates referred to the visits at the K homes and the comforting boredom of signing off the reports. I thought of the second advocate I had spoken to, his urbane manner and easy authority... and then I remembered the outburst that had seemed to emerge from a different and little used part of his mind.

A House at the End of the Road

Several days later, I found myself driving through the Lancashire countryside. I had just left the motorway and, almost immediately, the roads narrowed into lanes that could hardly allow two cars to pass. I missed my turning and had to reverse to get into the half-hidden cul-de-sac that wound its way around the fields for about a mile and a half. When I finally arrived I noticed two houses set back from the road. I could only just see the chimney of the further house as it was hidden behind tall trees and a wooden fence. The other house was a double-fronted bungalow with what seemed to be a detached house in the back garden. I could just see the first floor of the house over the top of the bungalow roof.

After parking in the front drive I rang the doorbell. There was no answer so I knocked hard on the door. Both the porch door and the main door were closed so it was possible nobody inside could hear me. I pushed the bell again but there was no sound. It was already five past two and my meeting with the manager of the K programme was due to have started by now. Frustrated, I started to walk around the outside of the

16

bungalow and looked in through the front windows. I could see unusually tidy teenagers' bedrooms, both dominated by the red duvet covers and posters of Liverpool Football Club. Through the porch window I could see children's paintings but, unusually, they didn't seem to be pictures painted by the older children who I knew lived there but by younger ones, perhaps as young as three or four.

The gravel crunched under my feet as I walked up and down the front drive. My mobile rang a couple of times and I briefly dealt with other work until I saw a man climbing over a stile and then walking over with his dog. "Excuse me", I shouted, "Which one's O House?" He pointed to the bungalow.

"You have to bang as hard as you can but you probably won't get in. It's a bloody nightmare for the postman." I looked at the porch and then at the cars parked in the driveway - both with tinted rear windows.

"I've seen children playing here a few times," he said, nodding to a grassy area on the other side of the road. As he walked away, I watched the crows fly over and land on the newly-ploughed fields. I waited for another half an hour and was just about to leave when I heard the sound of a car engine and tyres crunching on the gravel. It was the manager J. in a new red Mini.

I could see through the windscreen that she was about 50 and tanned. When she climbed out of her car she seemed slightly out of breath and, as she tried to open the front door she exclaimed dramatically how she couldn't understand why there wasn't anyone at home. Even then I felt there was a coldness in her eyes and an evasiveness which I had already sensed in her emails and phone calls. I'd already decided that I would listen to her and let her talk, not show the slightest disapproval or any distaste even though I thought she might say things that

17

were abhorrent. I would play ignorant and try to let her give me as much information as possible.

In the end, after a lot of banging on doors and windows we got in her car and she took me to a busy cafe in a farmers market. I was afraid she wouldn't be as candid in such a public place but it turned out that the noise stopped anyone from overhearing and she told me everything.

"So what do you want to know?" she asked.

"I just need to know how we can best support you. I know I haven't been that good about getting the quarterly figures in recently and I just need to know if there is anything I can do at the moment to help."

I could see her relax. The almost comical shifting of her eyes from side to side stopped and she started to see me as a co-conspirator.

"How many children have you got in the homes?" I asked.

"Altogether?"

"Yes."

"We've got 40 in the 11 Attachment Homes. We've got homes all over the country but those eleven are the only ones where we use holding therapy."

"How old are they, the kids?"

"There's a range, from eight to eighteen. Most of the homes are three- to four-bedded but we've got one which is larger - that's the one where some of the younger children live".

"So what does the therapy actually involve?" I asked. "I've read the chapter from *The Extra Dimension*. Is that what happens in the therapy?" *The Extra Dimension* was a book written by one of the founders of the K programme. In a filing cabinet at Head Office, I'd found a photocopied chapter detailing the therapy process step by step. The descriptions were consistent with the Evergreen models of holding therapy and, among other things, included the need to "deliberately distress the child" within therapy.

"Yeah, that's basically what we do. That's it."

As we sat in the cafe, among the tweedy middle-class pensioners and efficient black-clad waitresses, it occurred to me how surreal this was. We were talking about these practices that seemed to belong to a different world and next to us middle England was sipping tea from bone china cups and discussing the weather.

As the buzz of conversation continued, J. efficiently told me about the practicalities of the programme. "There are 40 children, all having weekly therapy for no less than two years. If they refuse, then it lasts longer. There is education in house and it's a strict no-no for family members to visit the homes." She continued with a clipped rat-a-tat-tat of facts. Over the next half an hour I learnt that Ofsted was responsible for the governance (even though I could find no reference to holding therapy in any of its reports). Each of the children is taken weekly to a single therapy centre in the NH Business Park in Rossendale in order to undergo the therapy, sometimes for several hours at a time.

She described the confusion around the ownership of the K programme and helped me understand the different names under which the company was listed. Taking a deep breath, she said that the programme was bought by a much larger Irish company called B in 2006. This company changed its entire name to K but the 11 Attachment Homes retained their unique identity. After the sale, SF, one of the founders of K was employed as a consultant. "She got her money and buggered off" said J. SF is still the only trainer of therapists the K Programme has ever had.

Does anybody else do holding therapy in the country? I asked. J. shook her head "No, nobody that will admit it anyway."

The day after this meeting I flew to Spain on holiday with my family. We stayed on the Costa del Sol in a friend's flat, not far from Malaga. A path led from the garden and, after a gentle climb over green and blue shrub-covered dunes, the ground sloped down towards the Mediterranean and away from the sound of cicadas. In the evenings we had collected firewood for the barbecue and sat on the porch listening to the waves in the distance. During this time I thought about the strangeness of what I had learnt over the last week. Every morning I woke up and expected everything suddenly to make sense. There must be some explanation, or at least an excuse. The debate must have been played out before and the whole thing justified in some way. Yet, every time I got out of bed and opened the sliding doors that led to the garden I was still faced with the same awful sense that something terribly wrong was happening.

At the end of August the sun was too hot for us to do anything apart from stay in the shade of our garden. To pass the time I read many of the books that could be found in the flat. Among these I found William Shirer's *Rise and Fall of the Third Reich*, Anne Applebaum's *Gulag* and Kazuo Ishiguro's *Never Let me Go*. Shirer's book was illustrated with photographs and I remember a particular scene in which, after the allied victory, local families were made to walk through the concentration camps.

When the holiday finished, I passed on all the information

about the K programme to my organisation. I remember there being many debates, long e-mails and a meeting with the Chief Executive. Finally, after all this, I was suspended. I had argued, after many discussions with a senior lawyer at the charity that this was potentially a criminal matter and the police should be informed. They disagreed and, for this reason only, I was escorted out of the building. I immediately went to the nearest police station and was put in touch with Detective Superintendent C, Head of Public Protection at Lancashire Police. I was relieved to discover that he took the allegations very seriously. Much later, after a meeting with Detective Inspector C, at Rossendale police station I sent both officers a letter.

Dear Detective Inspector C,

Further to our meeting on 18.9.10 I would like to re-emphasise my main concerns.

A key aspect of my decision to report this matter to the police was the evidence presented to me that informed consent had not been sought or received from the children and young people undergoing this therapy. Further to this, evidence had been presented to me that the Local Authorities placing the children with Sandringham had not been fully informed as to the nature of the therapy and therefore were unable to give meaningful consent to a highly intrusive and controversial treatment. After a number of discussions with a senior solicitor it was felt that this constituted evidence of assault and battery perpetrated within a highly systematic programme involving almost all the children within the eleven homes...

The police investigation continued for several months, until just before Christmas, and then closed. Inspector C. had said that without a survivor of the therapy there was no way the police could continue to investigate. Even though the head of the homes had told me first-hand that this was going on, the police still needed a former resident to report a crime. How was this going to happen? The whole nature of the treatment seemed to be focused on breaking down the children, to subjugate them to the authority of the therapist. So how on earth would a survivor be able to make statements to the police and lawyers against the very people who were treating them? The Inspector said there had never been a survivor who had made a statement to the police since the programme had started 14 years ago. There had been hundreds of children who had been through this, so what was the chance of this happening now?

The answer came through the internet.

First Contact

The internet allows the ordinary person to conduct research in a way in which only specialists were able to in the past. It helped me in two different ways. First, I was able to read almost all the literature on the subject. Most of the articles from US psychology journals were available in some form or other and large chunks of key books such as Professor Jean Mercer's *The Death of Candace Newmaker* and Rachael Stryker's *The Road to Evergreen* were also available. The internet also allowed me to discuss the treatment with American academics such as Monica Pignotti and follow the defamation trial that followed the lawsuit by US therapist, Ronald Federici.

Above all the internet allowed me to look for people who had been through the treatment. In the US, a website named Search for Survivors was dedicated to finding people who had gone through holding therapy. It was set up by a survivor who called herself Wayward Radish (a "Radish" was a derogatory term used by practitioners and others to describe a young person diagnosed with Reactive Attachment Disorder (RAD) – the primary condition now treated by holding therapy.) By the time it was closed down by its founder, the site had posted accounts of 11 survivors of the treatment, all of whom described severe abuse by attachment therapists.

In England, however, there was nothing. Extensive searches of the internet and the literature failed to find a single first-hand account of holding therapy, either positive or negative. The prospects of finding someone at this stage didn't look good.

This all changed in February 2011. I had started a blog called Invisible England in order to raise awareness of the issue and written two posts which generally discussed the background material. I had also started corresponding with Jean Mercer, Emeritus Professor of Psychology at Richard Stockton College in the United States. She had recently written an article which was highly critical of holding therapy. *The British Journal of Social Work* had accepted this for publication, after numerous changes had been made on the advice of its lawyers. Jean also felt that the crucial moment in the UK would come when a survivor was found who could speak about his or her experiences.

On the face of it, the task should not have been difficult. The internet is everywhere, everyone uses Facebook and Twitter and the power of Google searches would surely come up with someone who wanted to tell their story. In spite of this, search after search came up with nothing. Every possible combination of search terms led to the most obscure parts of the internet but nothing came up which could lead us to a survivor.

I was on the verge of giving up hope when we had our first breakthrough. A combination of search terms led to a deleted blog. Someone had written what could be identified as four posts but everything apart from the titles had been deleted. And yet, as I discovered by accident, there was a possibility these posts could be recovered. The cached (frozen) copy of one of the blogs was still available and, although I didn't yet know his name, it was through this route that I met David for the very first time. In some ways it was a ghostly encounter and there were many lost sentences but his words rang true even here. He had written:

ATURDAY, 27 NOVEMBER 2010

CHILD ABUSE OR THERAPY?
I am going to talk about one session i remember in particular

I walked into therapy I lay down my head on one therapist and my legs and feet on the other
i was asked to place behind behind SF's hand over the top of mine therapist B

placed her hands on my feet
back to prevent me from moving SF placed her hand over my mouth i tried to get away then my legs were also restrained to stop me from getting away and they would laugh between each other as if it was a joke putting me in this distress they would say things   ggb
t get reaction's like is this what daddy used to do it was like there down and now even now i have flash backs to
cared child and looking back now as an adult i truly think what they did to me in those therapy sessions was child abuse and
I am going to close for now but will be updating daily
Posted by **lifesfullofem** at 18:16
Email ThisBlogThis!Share to TwitterShare to FacebookShare to Google Buzz

I was given great encouragement by this find. It seemed to me that this was the first time someone had felt strong enough to write on the internet about their experiences. There had been some combination of factors and circumstance to allow this person to speak out. Professor Mercer still wasn't sure. I couldn't understand this at the time as I felt that, although we didn't have a name, it was unlikely that this was an imposter. Later it occurred to me that many years of challenging the practice in the US had taught her to be cautious.

The initial breakthrough was followed by intense frustration. The other deleted posts had all been completely lost and all that was left were the tantalisingly surreal titles of the posts. A month passed and nothing further happened until I logged into Facebook and searched for "attachment therapy" in combination with other terms. A group called "The K Programme, Child Abuse or Therapy?" then appeared, with a single member who appeared to be appealing for former residents. I wrote a message to the author and it was here that I encountered someone using the name Nikky Jackson.

From the moment I started writing to him I knew this was the same person who had started the blog. The writing was unmistakable and the lack of punctuation seemed only to emphasise the genuineness of his personality.

I asked what he/she knew about K.

"What's your connection with them?" came the reply.

I told him. He told me his real name was David and that he had been placed in one of the K. homes between the ages of 11 and 13. He was reluctant to tell me more - I knew he wanted to but it seemed that experience had told him to be extremely wary. I didn't blame him. I was a stranger asking him about the most intimate aspects of his life. Why should he tell me anything? He asked me if he could call me at work to check me out. He wrote:

> Yes it hard to trust people while talking about
> these issues and i do have a bit of anxiety
> meeting as i dont know who your are
> but yet again i have a great passion to get this
> out in the public domain but i feel that i have to
> have some sort check to say who you say you
> are please don't feel offended by my air of
> caution i have just searched the the GSCC
> register where you do appear would you allow
> me to ring you at your place of work just to put
> my mind 100% at rest i would not discuss
> anything we have talked about just ring the
> switch bord and ask for you
> i am sorry to ask this as you are probley say
> who you say your and really honest nice person
> but after you have been what i have been
> through its always good to check once my mind
> is at rest i will meet ASAP
>
> with regards David

He rang and asked for me at the switchboard but was told he had to tell them who he was. At the second attempt he was put through and the sound of his voice made him impossibly real. It was like a character from a novel calling me up on the telephone.

Once we had spoken he started to open up. The switchboard connection had been a symbolic moment and he sent me many e-mails after this, each one longer and more personal than the next. I also think he instinctively felt that I understood the whole idea of holding therapy and everything that it meant for him.

27

> …just so glad there is some one out there in
> the uk who understands and gets it!!!!! such
> a rare thing to come across

He asked me about my background and what my connection was to the K programme. I told him that I didn't work for them and was interested only in raising awareness of the therapy. He replied:

> I will be so glad to help you with this as for
> the K group they are very clever but as
> years after the inital therapy i was fosterd by
> the director of K. and have seen the
> bussiness from the other side if you will
> i also have ex staff i am in contact with i
> recently an email from an current member
> of staff yesterday stating the was K therapy
> was used was wrong… i have so much
> useful infomation i think would benifit you
> for instance when i was 11 i used to bite as a
> kid and is was decided when i was
> restrained i rubber dog bone would be
> forced into my mouth in my mind thats
> abuse a bg investigationb was done socal
> services police but they got away with it
> beacuse is was called a therpy
> approach!!!!!!!! mad i will close for now i
> am at your disposal i will be making a trip
> up north in june i will keep you posted on
> that and maybe we can meet then but in the
> meantime i feel it is important to to
> move this forward so what i ever i can do
> thorugh email corrospondence i will
> certainly get on with it

> finally some one in the uk who finally
> understands this is wrong

He felt that I understood him, or at least I understood that part of him. I felt this too and wondered why this was the case. Perhaps it was because I was a social worker and had often worked with vulnerable people. On the other hand, he later said there were lots of social workers, and for that matter, lots of therapists, psychologists and lawyers who were also trained up in that way but didn't seem to understand. It's still a mystery but, strangely enough, a part of me believes that living in Russia at a certain time in its history helped me to relate to him. It hadn't been long since it was a totalitarian state and there was a feeling that society was at a tipping point, the point at which it was beginning to dawn on people just how every aspect of their lives had been controlled. Oppression is oppression wherever it is experienced and whatever its scale. Perhaps that's why I seemed to understand where he was coming from - who knows?

Right from the beginning I had had a question to which I needed to know the answer. What did the therapy involve? The question was crucial because Sudbery et al had been very vague about what took place during the sessions. As Jean had written, this was problematic because it was left wide-open for anybody to claim this paper as justification for there practices. There was a general feeling that the aggressive Evergreen model operated only in the USA and that it is just not something we would do in the UK. To ask David this was a delicate matter and I needed to wait until the right moment. I think it was about week after my first contact with him that he wrote me the most powerful and expressive e-mail I have ever received. On 5 April 2011 I received the following:

> The Therapy sessions them selves were
> quite traumatic

One other adult usally one of the unit
residential staff   had to lie down feet on the
one adult who would then hold the feet
down on the top half one hand behind the
therapist back been held by the person sat
next to her one hand place on my chest held
down my the therapist and constant forced
eye to eye contant if i looked way my head
would have been pinned in the direction of
the therapist and if i tried to say no another
hand would firmly clasped over my mouth
which would send me into a fit of rage all
this was also backed up with alot of shouting
and swearing the therapist would say things
like is this what your fucking birth mum did
to you did she and the hand would come of
my mouth for a responce this seemed to go
on for ages
in the end i was so drained and broken and
scared i just said yes in therapy i was
constanly prevented from rubbing my eye if
i had an itch prevented from stretching
prevented from doing all nataural that i
human being does to relive a discomfort and
sureley that is taking away a basic human
right
but at the end of each session broken tired it
was kind of drilled in that all this was ok and
they always managed to manipulate you to
feeling ok when you left the session. another
time i was wrapped in a blankett pind down
and held so tight all i could feel was fright
so i responded again with agression looking
back this is what they wanted break you

down to comply. i also attented so called
intensive therapy where there would be 2
therapist again pinned down basicly given
torrents of abuse poked proded until i
reached agression again. I was i liveley lad
growing up always trying to push boundries
but during my time at K i turned into this
agressive monster attacked so many staff bit
them punched them hit i had many bruises
from this place and sometimes looked quite
ill and run down i kept getting told they
would help me but infact it was there
methods that were turning me into somthing
else in one instance i had splints put on my
arms to imobilise me then they woud start
laughing at amd humiliating me and again i
went into a rage put power less as i was
splinted in the end my violence got so out of
contol i as kicking off every day staff were
hospitalised in the end it was decided K
couldnt meet my needs due to the increase in
violent behaviour which now but that is
what they turned me into after meeting and
meeting its was decided i should go into a
secure unit but then at the last second S. said
i want to foster this boy my therapist and
director of K. fostering well that is a
different story for years in the placement
with them was ruled by fear and attachment
therapy was never mentioned in her home
she would bring kids back from work and
make them sleep on the stairs on the floor
and make them look after her disabled son
who would often beat them up just to make
them apprciate there own home this therapy

31

is not about helping children its about making a child love or attach through fear! i tried to tell my head teacher in the late 90's about what was going on she seemed concerned but again K. and S. got away with it and i got the biggest bollocking of my life. as for the staff in the units them selves were taken young carers with no experience been manipulated to work the K way alot have staff have left as they felt this was wrong and one member of staff in my defence reported the dog bone incident and also reported doctoring of K logs to put K in a better light which i have in my social services records whilst in the care of K and S to my knolledge never had an inderpendent evaluation until i was 14 when i went to the priory with S to be assed which was not inderpendent as the doctor was a freind of Ss once these people have these children in there care its kept very close to K the ouside world was totally oblivious to what was going on in my mind as social workers didnt understand the practices now i am left with anixety and never 100% trust anyone i am rid with guilt i feel stupid as i said am trying another therapy through the NHS to fix all the crap S. and Ks attachment did to me

i hope this is ok for starters if there is any direct question you wish to ask please do so as i do seem to rambble on some what

So there it was - a first-hand account of the therapy used in the K Programme.

Could this be what they did to some of the most vulnerable children in the country? Nobody can deny that there is a descriptive power in these words that make you think that they cannot be anything but honest. In fact, more than that, the words seem so heartfelt it seems as if he is actually there again and re-living it when he writes it. The lack of punctuation, the misspellings, these only heighten the expression of emotion through a kind of stream -of-consciousness that comes from deeply-buried memory. I've asked him to describe this again verbally several times since he sent me this and, although the accounts are entirely consistent, nothing matches the power of the original. It's as if he feels that he has expressed it here in the best way he could and that this is his testimony.

There were so many questions that I wanted to ask. First of all, he was fostered by his therapist. How could this be ethical? Everything in my experience told me that this would be an unacceptable conflict of interests. Also, if he went through the therapy and then later lived with the person who did these things, how had he managed to survive? These were questions that I asked him in my next e-mails and he asked if he could write about this the next day – it was becoming obvious that the effort of remembering was extremely painful.

Later that night he sent me an account of foster placement with the head of therapy at K:

> The situation surrounding me going to S and As
>
> I was highly aggressive within there childrens homes and it was said to be decided my the staff team that the could no longer work with me so an order for me to be placed into a secure until was made in the 11th hour Ss.

husband said he had seen me in one of the homes when he was there carrying out maitinance work

And said S. and him self would foster but looking back this was all set up by S. using A. as the front man. It was the summer holidays when I went there I was told I was having a break from k but soon after told I would be going back I had fun for the first few weeks I was bought toys clothes computers days out and was given the freedom of any normal kid I also managed to secure a place at an EBD school in b. where I would be a week resident and go to A and S at weekends I started school and got in to the routine the support from the school was amazing at weekends a typical weekend was cleaning the house and looking after Ss profoundly disabled son A and S were compleat control freaks I still talk my ex foster sister now and we resent them so much for loss of out child hood. In the house hold there were 8 other children adopted all but one had some sort of disability S always tried to make her self look like the model mother to the out side world she was perfect a role model respected and she knew it and used to lord it over us constantly she hated if we talked to anyone out of the family she hated us having friends its like to wanted to protect what she had built up in her home I myself made the mistake of talking to my head teacher at school about things that were upsetting me ie children been brought back from K to be made to sleep on the stairs on the floor no cover just the clothes they had on there back I told my head teacher about K and what they did and that weekend I went back to A and S I got the biggest bollocking of my life She went beserk you don't tell anyone not anyone about what goes on in my house or what happened at K do you hear me and then would try and start to manipulate me with her fake tears I soon cotton on to that one S famous fake tears as time went on I started to miss behave at school so I wouldn't have to go home at the weekends to look after her disabled son and clean am not saying it was all cleaning and baby sitting I mean we had all the gadjets is was like you can have these nice things but there were always a price pay one Friday I had missed behaved at school on purposes so my punish ment would be that I wanst allowed home I was in turmoil S. turned up at school I was scared but she managed to get at me and filled me full of false promises so then I went home after about 2 years S. came and said I want you to change your name to F. and told me to tell my social worker as really controlled well we also attended church and she said she would buy me an armarni shirt if I was baptized into the catholic faith and at that age well yes easily perueded so I did. Shortly later A. was diagnosed with ME he got extreamly angry and violent many time with all us kids at one point of another it was like livng on egg shells most of the time. On one occasion one of S sons with learning disabiltues dropped some food on the floor he wanted to put it in the bin

but she swept up the rest of the kitchen and
made him hear the food he had dropped on the
floor and muck S loved humiliating and contol
at the age of 15 I refused to go home again and
was put into a childrens home in preston for
the night but I got so much shit of social
workers and the care staff saying how
wondefull Sa was I just give up and went
back can you imagin how hard it is to prove a
women is a abuser when she is this pioneering
therapist company director and I am just some
skank kid in care something just died in side
me at 16 I ran way from home as A was
verbally assaulting me every day gay boy and
other names and once some occasion pushed
me around so I ran away again to my ex foster
dad who I was with b4 I went into K but
again told to go back but this time I didn't I
went out on my own got my own house years
later some one got in contact with me and
said S wants to talk to you so I thought I
would call to see what she had to say I took
my partner to meet them and they ripped me
to shreds your useless stupid my partner to this
day says every time we used to see them I
used to turn into a quiver dumb wreck the
biggest thing that hurts me is S. forced me to
chuck all my baby photos and passed life
down a gap in the house when they were
doing a loft conversion so in that house is my
passed life just sat in the dust she stole my
identity she stole my child hood she was
allowed to abuse me as a therapist as a mother
because every one thought she was great and
there is fuck all I can do about because I still

36

feel like that stupid powerless kid who carnt
make the world she what she and her therapy
has done to me she has in my eyes made her
self invinsable there are so many things to say
but writing them all would take soooo long I
hope this gives you a bit of an insight if there
is anything else you need to know just mail
me I hope this s ok for you and to be honest it
hurt so much writing this and brought back so
many flash backs and memories but also long
as I keep telling myself its for a good cause it
will keep me strong

David

The previous e-mail had provided a description of the
treatment itself but this new message gave real insight into the
motivations of the head therapist and the co-founder of the
programme. The descriptions of the household highlight the
apparent obsession with creating a completely controlled
environment and the various methods used to maintain this.
Particularly poignant was the passage in which David is made
to throw his baby photographs down a gap in the house while
a loft conversion was being completed – "so in that house is
my past life just sat in the dust she stole my childhood she
stole my identity she stole my child hood". What is just as
disturbing is that this person was also in control of what was
termed an "adoption support service" charged with enabling
the transition to adoption for hundreds of children in care.

In a way this is a key issue. It is clearly the case that adoption
is by far the best option for many children in care, it gives
them a security and stability that would otherwise be hard to
achieve. The difficulty comes when children have an
attachment to a birth parent which must be carefully and
sensitively considered. It can't just be thrown away. One of

the principles of holding therapy is that the birth parent is often talked about highly negative terms and, indeed, this is one of the methods used to provoke children during the therapy sessions. It must be said that to treat children in this way runs counter to every evidence-based theory in child psychiatry.

After reading these accounts I wondered what the social workers view of all this was. David said that he had been given a CD containing some of his social services records. I later found out that there were quite a few gaps but a few days after he sent me his account of the foster placement he sent me a letter of complaint from his files. He then wrote:

> Yea i think it was a worker at K who but a complaint i will keep looking through all my files i have on K would it help if i sent you all the K and social work corrsponence? and therapy notes? i know these are personel to me but i am ok about sharing for the pupose of what you and i are trying to achive it may help if you wish me to do so i will compile them all into a work document and send them to you. The is a worker who is now a manager at K who did put a complaint in all them years ago who i dont think would talk openly to anyone else but me regarding the past but the abuse didnt stop with the kids in a way this particular member of staff in a therapy was asked do you love this child meaning me she replied yes and the therapist shouted back no you fucking dont and the carer got quiet upset but i do then the therapist proceeded to ask her if there was a fire and your kids were in it and David who would you rescue first carer said my kids therpaist replies there you go you dont

38

love   this   child!
as hard as it was the member of staff to hear
this imagine me as a child thinking that the
people who were suposed to keep me safe didnt
love me another feeling of rejection?!

A real mystery was how so many people who worked
for the organisation had been complicit in participating
in or remaining silent about it. It seemed that the junior
staff were also coerced or bullied. Yet, as David
himself says, if the staff felt under pressure then how
did the children feel?

Voices from the Past

As things became clearer and I began to think about all the information I was getting from the research, from David, from JH and from other sources, it became clearer to me just how systematic the K programme was. The 40 children seemed to be mainly subject to Care Orders or Interim Care Orders. This means that they had been through the court process and had been discussed in many meetings involving social workers, teachers, health professionals etc. They had been seen by solicitors, barristers and guardian ad litems and had expert reports written about them by psychologists and psychiatrists.

On top of this was the money involved. Their time in the programme will have been paid for by public funds from health, education and social care. From my own experience at various funding panels. I knew that residential placements often cost several thousand pounds a week per child. Given all the services on offer at the K. programme, this meant that it was very likely that millions of pounds of public money had been spent on a highly- intrusive treatment which few people had ever heard of. In order to understand this worrying situation I decided to research the origins of holding therapy in the US and in the UK.

A good case can be made for saying that holding therapy in the US has its roots in an experimental treatment called Rage-reduction Therapy or the Z-process. This treatment was developed by an American psychiatrist called Robert Zaslow in the 1960s and 1970s and involved "physically holding a child to confront and work through rage and motor resistance to create a positive relationship with the therapist". In Z-process Therapy it was proposed that the therapist should "incite rage in the child in order to work through intense emotions and to learn how to express them healthily and at appropriate times". This was in- line with the "feeling therapy" that existed in the 1970s that argued that that the patient needed to re-experience the trauma in order to be cured. It was openly expressed by its proponents that Zaslow's methods were "intentionally intrusive, confrontational, physical and lengthy".

At the time he was practising many other experimental therapies were being developed, such as William Reich's Orgone Therapy and Jacqui Schiff's version of Eric Berne's Transactional Analysis which regressed patients to their childlike state in order to purge them of their early trauma. It was in this atmosphere that Zaslow was able to treat hundreds of children before he was eventually investigated for professional misconduct and discredited. It was in 1972 that the State of California revoked his licence on the grounds that he was conducting "dangerous and reckless therapy that caused serious injury to a patient" and, following this, it is thought he never practised or published on the subject again.

However, although Zaslow disappeared from the scene in the early 1970s his ideas were adopted by a therapist called Foster

Cline. Cline adapted the Z-process by adding elements of psychoanalysis and wrote in 1979 that Zaslow was, in his view, an unappreciated genius. Cline set up "Evergreen Consultants in Human Behaviour" in the town of Evergreen, Colorado and later set up the Attachment Centre at Evergreen, treating hundreds of emotionally disturbed children there. According to Cline, a typical Rage-Reduction Therapy session was conducted as follows:

> I lay the child on my left so that his body is stretching out to my right. The child's head is cradled in my left arm. I may hold the child's left arm up and around the top of his head. Thus his own left arm forms a cradle for his head and restrains it, and this position leaves my right hand free to play "spider" or lovingly poke him around his ribs and tummy. One way or another the child's legs have to be restrained so they cannot kick the therapist or other furniture in the room. This may take other people, or sometimes we can restrain their legs with one of our own. With my free hand I can also open the child's eyelids, to force eye contact, or close his mouth when I don't like what he is saying. Essentially the therapist controls the placement and quantity of tactile stimulation, with his right free hand, varying it a little from a "fun little spider" burrowing into the navel or the subclavicular space, to a somewhat abrasive, rubbing stimulation on the ribcage. When the child is not being worked with extensively through touch , his labyrinthine (inner ear) mechanisms may be stimulated by sitting him up, turning his head etc. All of this varied high-intensity stimulation is designed to break up the child's habitually rigid and stereotyped responses.

> He is not allowed to use his usual repetitive auto-stimulatory mechanisms such as rubbing his lips scratching himself, hitting himself making repetative vocalisations, etc.

It is difficult to imagine how Cline managed to practise in this way with so few checks and little professional oversight. In any case, he generally operated under the radar throughout the 1980s until he came to the attention of the authorities after the death of a 13-year-old girl called Andrea Swenson. Swenson had been undergoing holding therapy at the Attachment Centre at Evergreen (ACE) and had been placed with therapeutic foster carers employed by ACE. While in their care, she had been violently ill and incoherent during the night and breathing heavily and vomiting the next morning. However her foster carers had then gone bowling and left her alone. She was later found dead from an aspirin overdose in her carers' house. The case was settled out of court but Cline later voluntarily gave up his licence after a separate holding-therapy-related incident at the Attachment Centre.

After Cline ceased working as a therapist, holding therapy continued to be used in a number of clinics at Evergreen but continued to avoid attention from mainstream child psychiatry. It was promoted by word of mouth and through the internet and, as the anthropologist Rachael Stryker has described, relied on appeals to homespun folklore rather than on evidence from properly conducted research.

The next person to make use of holding therapy was a psychiatrist called Martha Welch. Welch advocated the use of holding therapy as a treatment for autistic children and had developed her theories on the now discredited view that Autism stemmed from attachment difficulties with the mother. She described her theories in a book called *Holding Time* and, for a time, her ideas gained popularity – with holding therapy clinics being set up, mainly in the US but also a few in Europe. Welch's treatment involved a form of compression therapy that:

> instructed mothers to take hold of their children during defiant periods, holding them to the point of inducing anger. Therapists told mothers that the child may spit, scream, swear, attempt to get free, bite and try to cause alarm by saying he is in pain, cannot breathe, will vomit, is going to die, or need to urinate. With Welch's approach, parents were encouraged to accept these behaviours calmly and silently. Welch described a subsequent stage (marked by a child's weeping and wailing) in which parents were encouraged to resist the temptation to feel sorry for the child or feel guilty about what they were doing. Therapists were told that if they could successfully resist these temptations, the child would enter an acceptance state in which the child would fight less and become relaxed and tired. The therapist then instructed the mother to loosen her hold on the child, at which point a bonding process was believed to begin, in which the child would find comfort from the mother in this relaxed state

It is possible to see the attraction in such a theory. There is an appeal to popular ideas of struggle and catharsis and a focus on the need to tolerate immediate discomfort in order to achieve longer–term benefits. On the other hand, it is also not difficult to predict the potential dangers of this approach. The automatic dismissal of a child's expressions of pain and distress leaves the child in an emotional cul-de-sac and could lead to risks of accidental injury or the possible exploitation of this vulnerability.

As Rachel Stryker points out the use of Welch's methods began to wane when it became clear that the treatment could not be empirically demonstrated to work on autistic children. Like Cline, Welch operated under the radar until her methods came under fire following the death of a 10-year-old child from North Carolina. Candace Newmaker was suffocated during a therapy session conducted by an Evergreen therapist called Connell Watkins.

Candace Newmaker's death in 2000 was probably the most dramatic example of the dangers of holding therapy. For me, the reason why it is useful to study this case is that it throws light on the motivations and ways of thinking that are related to the use of holding therapy around the world.

At the time of her death Candace was being treated by Watkins in order to help her bond with her adoptive mother, Jeane Newmaker. Watkins used a form of holding therapy called rebirthing therapy and this involved Candace being wrapped up tightly in a blanket, which symbolised the birth canal, and forced to struggle out of the blanket in order to be "re-born". During this process Newmaker repeatedly cried out that she was losing control of her bodily functions and that she was suffocating to death. These cries were ignore by the therapists and, 70 minutes later she died. The whole process was videotaped by the therapists and subsequently shown in full at the trial.

It seems that this evidence and the case as a whole had a significant effect on the people attending the trial. Jeanette Bartha, who attended the trial was profoundly shocked by the evidence, particularly by the videotapes, and campaigns on the issue to this day. Another person who attended the trial was Professor Jean Mercer.

Professor Mercer had read about holding therapy in a social work text book in about 1996 and became interested in a treatment that was being used but not discussed in the mainstream literature. After some initial research into the subject she learned about Candice Newmaker's death. After reading the initial reports, Professor Mercer decided to attend the trial hearings and acted as a consultant on the case. She later wrote about her experiences of the trial in *Attachment Therapy on Trial: the Torture and Killing of Candace Newmaker*. As a child psychologist she discussed, within the book, the errors of reasoning that lead to such tragedy being allowed to take place.

Following the trial and the publication of the book Professor Mercer became involved with the organisation called Advocates for Children in Therapy, founded by campaigners Linda Rosa and Larry Sarner. This group recently became caught up in a lawsuit by Ronald Federici, a prominent therapist involved with the treatment of adoptees from the former Soviet Union. The lawsuit was eventually dismissed but not without Professor Mercer and her colleagues paying substantial costs.

It was during the trial that I first began to correspond with Jean. She had recently written an article in the *British Journal of Social Work* that had severely criticised an eight-year-old, privately commissioned, study into the K programme that had just been published. She was awaiting a reply from Sudbery et al, who had written the original paper so, when I told her that I had made contact with a former resident at K, she was immediately interested. When I sent her his "First-hand Account of Holding Therapy" she instinctively knew that this "remarkable and disturbing account" was clear evidence that the worst sort of US-style holding therapy was taking place within the K programme.

Another important academic who has written about Holding Therapy is Professor Rachael Stryker, author of the *The Road to Evergreen*. Although this book was published as recently as 2010 it was based on a doctoral thesis that drew upon research undertaken in the late 1990s. Stryker, an anthropologist, became interested in the fate of Russian adoptees who had arrived in the US following the collapse of the Soviet Union. As a result of this, she began to follow a group of therapists operating in the Evergreen area of Colorado who had started working with these adoptees. Her book describes the work of these therapists with these children and uses interviews with children, their carers and the therapists. She was able to observe at first-hand many of the therapy sessions.

Stryker's book discusses the importance of social status for many of the adoptive parents which was often prioritised above the needs of the children. The need to be seen as a good and responsible parent, and therefore a respected member of the community, seemed to trump any considerations in relation to the innate well-being of the child. Although the book uses information that was collected some time ago it contains invaluable information about the modus operandi of many of the therapists.

Meeting David

So what would David be like? I looked at my watch and saw that I would be meeting him in less than three hours. My main worry was that he might not turn up. This would not at all have been surprising given that he had described his most personal experiences to me and might be regretting it. He had learnt to be very cautious about trusting people and it would have been a logical reaction to want to close up again having opened up so much.

The thing that fascinated me about him was what it was that had enabled him to survive. Actually, not only to survive but to survive with his personality so intact that he had been able to tell his story with such clarity. As I was to find out, others had experienced similar things, so why had nobody else come forward? The answer to this that comforts the proponents of the programme is that there is no one else who experienced it in this way. Yet, because even the most superficial investigation will show that many others have suffered in the same way, the answer must be that everything about the treatment acts against the survivor remaining intact enough to tell his or her story.

On the way down to see him I changed trains at Birmingham and then at Bristol and when I arrived at the station in Taunton I was faced with the fact that there were two exits. To my shame I considered the thought that David had decided not to come. I knew that if he *did* turn up it would be a remarkable feat of courage – to have experienced many years of not being easily able to trust anyone and then to face meeting a social worker whom he had never seen and then a partner in a large law firm that he had never even spoken or written to. I chose an exit and waited at a bus stop a few metres away. He had wanted to pick me up in his car. I had been pleased about this as it offered him a degree of control over the proceedings. Much of what had happened so far had been initiated by others and he needed to feel an equal partner in what we were about to do.

When he drove up I knew it was him, even through the misted up windscreen. He recognised me as well. I got into his car and shook his hand. There was a sense of relief that I couldn't quite explain at first – perhaps because I had thought he might not come. It was partly this but I think it was a sense I had when I spoke to him that he was exactly as I had expected him to be. We drove away from the station without knowing really where we were going. It was still too early to meet with the lawyer so he decided to drive me to his local village. On the face of it this seemed like a good idea but it became clear after a few miles that we were going to struggle to get back in time. We decided halfway to stop for a coffee by the side of the main road at a burger van. There were a couple of wooden benches on the lay-by, so it was there that we were first able to talk.

He was nervous of course. Not only was he meeting me for the first time but he was due to see a partner in a large law firm. He smoked continuously and came across as matey. His joshing was a genuine attempt to be friendly, to make a connection, but also seemed like strategy to protect himself.

We talked about his family - he had two young children who had just started primary school. He had met his partner when he was 17 and in a homeless hostel. He was, without question, lucky. He could have met anyone in that hostel and could have fallen in with a group that would have been dysfunctional in every way apart from the promise to be there for him when so many others were not. The fatal attraction of the gang or some other destructive relationship was probably a hazard that was narrowly avoided. As it was, it seems that he fell in love with somebody who had his best interests at heart and who, in the best possible way, needed his love as much as he need hers.

After two cups of coffee and four cigarettes we headed back into Taunton. There was a final cigarette outside the shiny new law offices of Foot Anstey and then a short wait in reception.

Clair was a businesslike woman. She had recently been made a partner in the firm and had worked on a class action lawsuit within the Bristol Hospital heart scandal. It was difficult to work out who had broken this story but the main people involved seemed to have been an anaesthetist and a journalist at *Private Eye*. *Private Eye,* it seems, was keen to make amends after making a mess of the MMR scandal - it had given voice to the claims made by Dr Andrew Wakefield, a doctor who had been initially given credit for linking the vaccine to autism but was later discredited. It got it right, however, with the Bristol case and dozens of parents lined up to take legal action against the doctors who had incompetently treated their children. It was with this knowledge that we followed her into a leather- and chrome-filled meeting room, where David would again tell his story.

It was an awkward situation at first. David was anxious but full of hope that someone would finally listen to him. Clair, I sensed, was navigating unfamiliar territory. It was one thing pursuing a straightforward case of medical negligence, no matter how large-scale it was. This was different.

There had been no case law in the UK regarding this at all and there was no clear way it could be categorised. On top of this, David was less able to express himself to someone he had never met before. True, he had had contact with me for only a week or so before he started writing in detail about his history but I had corresponded with him in the preceding period and had spoken to him on the phone. The discussion with Clair was being entered into cold, without any run-up and in an unfamiliar and formal setting. He was being asked to gear himself up again and re-live the most traumatic events of his life. Unsurprisingly, he found this almost impossible to do.

On reflection it was incredible that he could describe as much as he did. It was an outline compared to the in depth accounts he had written in his e-mails. There was a sense that he was struggling with the fact that someone was finally listening and that he almost couldn't allow this to work. In some ways he didn't really make every effort to make himself appear sympathetic. Perhaps this was a part of his honesty, a way of being true to himself even if it led to unhelpful consequences.

A measure of his anxiety came when he got up to go to the toilet and returned almost before he had left. He opened the door breathless worried, he said, that we had spoken about him in his absence. The difficulty he had trusting people was a continual reminder of his past.

After David had given his statement Clair described the possible stages of the case. The first step was to get Legal Help, preliminary funding to get things off the ground. We then needed to see if we could get past the financial and legal hurdle of Legal Aid. If we got this, a case could have to be put together and, files requested from health, education and the K. Group. Independent experts would then be recruited to consider whether the therapy constituted abuse. Two years was the initial timescale and an estimate of £40,000 – £50,000 was predicted as the compensation if he was successful.

After two-and-a-half hours we stood in the car park, David smoking yet another cigarette. "Was it worth it?" I asked him. "Yes", he said, but I could see it had placed an enormous strain on him. At the station I asked him if he wanted to have a coffee before my train arrived. He said no, saying that his wife was waiting for him. The truth was he was completely drained.

More Voices from the Past

As already described, the starting point for Holding Therapy in the UK seems to have been when Martha Welch visited in the 1980s. However, when her theories became discredited and the use of Holding Therapy on autistic children declined, a small number of therapists also started to use the treatment on children diagnosed with Reactive Attachment Disorder - a rare condition associated with children who have experienced traumatic early childhoods.

By far the largest, most systematic and sophisticated programme of Holding Therapy in the UK began in about 1995 and was started in the north of England by a foster carer (S) and her social worker (B). The programme began as a non-profit making project but was soon reinvented into a private company. S, who for many years was the head of therapy, is now a consultant employed by the company. J, the current Managing Director of the Programme has stated that she remains the only trainer of therapists the company has ever had.

In 2001 the company commissioned Salford University to undertake an evaluation of its therapeutic practices. The university website records that it was paid £31,000 to undertake the study which consisted of a number of semi-structured interviews with staff and children. This study has never been publicly available and its findings were only published only eight years later, in the *British Journal of Social Work.*

Around the time of the report a number of articles appeared in the national press. These appeared simply to reproduce the claims of the company and failed to question, in any way, the nature of the therapy. There was even a feature on the BBC *Woman's Hour* which essentially seemed to advertise the service. However, after 2003 there were significantly fewer items in the media and by 2006 the company seems to have been in real financial trouble – items in local news papers confirm this. It may not be a coincidence that the, highly critical, BAAF Position Statement 4 appeared around this time.

The British Association of Adoption and Fostering is a large organisation, firmly placed within the mainstream of the British statutory child care framework. Its Chairman is Anthony Douglas, who is also head of the Child and Family Court Advisory Service. A recent trustee was Dame Elizabeth Butler-Sloss, formerly President of the Family Division.

In 2006 a report was published by the American Professional Society on the Abuse of Children (APSAC). This was a response to the growing concerns about Attachment/Holding Therapy in the US. The report was overwhelmingly critical of the treatment and raised concerns about its safety and efficacy. The BAAF position statement was also published in 2006 and raised very similar concerns. It appears that the publication of the two documents was motivated by very similar factors. The

BAAF statement, written by a senior manager, John Simmons, outlines the risks involved in Holding Therapy and describes, for example, the impossibility, inherent in such a treatment, of obtaining meaningful consent. The statement makes its point through the use of juxtaposition with the final paragraph warning of the dangers of institutional child abuse.

What happened soon after the publication of these statements was extensively recorded in the financial press and on the Companies House website. The K. Programme was bought by a much bigger parent company, based outside the country. The company's financial difficulties meant that this must have seemed like a last minute reprieve.

It was around this time that concerns were raised around private equity firms buying up small groups of children's homes and foster care companies in, what were called, "distressed sale" buyouts. A common theme was that these, sometimes family owned businesses, were being stripped of any elements that did not clearly contribute to the bottom line. The effect on the K Programme seemed to have been that the owners were much further removed from what was going on and may not have cared about it as long as it didn't affect the balance sheet. In fact, when I asked JH, the Managing Director about who supervised her, she said it was done by the Chief Financial Officer. She described the ritual that took place every morning when the group managers took part in a conference call with the CFO. "Each referral gained and lost was discussed – what got us the placement and what led to us losing one."

The buyout also led to some confusion about the extent of the programme and indeed its name. The larger company which bought the programme decided, for some reason to change its overall name to K. This nationwide organisation is a very large provider of children's homes so it is essential to clarify that not all these homes used Holding Therapy - HT continued to be used only by the original 11 K Attachment Homes in the north-west. This fact is something that cannot be discovered in the company's documentation. It is only because I had a direct connection with the company that I knew this. This lack of clarity may have proved useful to the company in terms of avoiding difficult questions if they arose. Unfortunately, few people seem to have wanted to ask these questions.

This is a theme that runs through this whole issue - that the people responsible for ensuring the safety and well-being of these children don't seem to have asked any questio ns but appear simply to have turned a blind eye. The Ofsted inspectors responsible for its governance don't even mention the words Holding Therapy or Attachment Therapy in any of their reports, the social workers don't seem even to know, or say they don't know, that this kind of therapy is taking place.

This vagueness and glossing over of things may not have seemed so terrible at the time but its cumulative effects appear to have been devastating..

As I was learning about the programme I constantly asked myself "why"? Why on earth would a group of people want to subject children to this treatment and why would the local authorities, who were responsible for the children, allow this to happen? Let's be clear here, responsibility for children in care means shared parental responsibility. There is a duty to be fully aware of any treatment the child is going through, especially if it is highly intrusive. In the event, few people spoke up, few people asked any difficult questions and there seems, for 16 years, to have been mainly silence.

From the beginning, it seemed that telling people about this was the most important thing to do. However, it was not that simple. The initial response from the independent advocates that I interviewed was frequently avoidance. When they were faced with what seemed to be going on, they responded with pleas of ignorance. So, if these advocates were professionally responsible for having knowledge of the programme, how would it be possible to raise it with others?

In general, the process of explaining the issue went something like this: the treatment would be generally described and there would be a period when the listener would try to digest the information and try to put into some sort of context. The trouble was there was very little within their experience to which they could compare it to. They would ask some questions and then search for some kind of appropriate response within themselves but, as it appeared to me, because they didn't really know how they were meant to react they didn't react at all. Better to ignore the whole thing than to feel something or think something they might regret later.

There is another barrier to communicating with people about Holding Therapy. It is the name itself that causes problems. The first word, "holding", cannot be more positive in its connotations. Images of love and care through physical contact are evoked: the mother holding her baby, the married couple who are given each other "to have and to hold". It is hard to think of the word as negative in any way.

The word "therapy" also has positive associations. Therapy, in many ways, is now seen as the modern panacea, curing all society's ills with only the length of the therapy a valid question when considering a positive outcome. It is difficult to consider that the two words together "Holding" and "Therapy" could describe anything other than something positive.

There are perhaps even greater problems with Holding Therapy's other name, "Attachment Therapy". The first

57

problem with this name is that it is often confused with attachment *theory,* the mainstream and universally accepted theory developed by John Bowlby, Mary Ainsworth and others. Apparently even some quite eminent professionals can confuse the two terms. Even if there is no confusion, the title produces strong expectations of a treatment that cannot be anything other than helpful. In many ways it was a real coup for these therapists to stake a claim to the term attachment therapy – how could anything with such an iconic name be anything other than based on long tradition of evidence-based research? In other words, the reality of attachment therapy is far removed from the positive images that are evoked by the name.

I was first alerted to these difficulties by Professor Jean Mercer, Emeritus Professor of Psychology at Richard Stockton University. Jean's help in the beginning was related to encouragement and describing the academic background. Later the help became more practical. A big question for David and me was whether he had a legal case or not. He had told me that, several years ago, he had tried to get help form a lawyer in Liverpool. The process had stalled, David said, because the lawyer simply "didn't get it". He had apparently expected some sort of sexual or, straightforward, physical abuse case. When David started to describe the treatment this entered territory that was completely unfamiliar and, as a consequence, the matter went no further. Cold-calling specialist law firms also failed to progress things for the same reason.

Then things changed. Jean had a connection with a barrister in Bristol with whom she had worked previously. This person identified a firm of solicitors specialising in class action lawsuits – they had recently worked on the Bristol Hospital heart scandal. It seemed that the personal connection was everything. When I rang them up and later sent them some literature, they invited me for an initial interview in their barristers' chambers. This three-hour discussion then led to a further meeting being set up in their Taunton offices with David - something that would cause David a great deal of excitement and anxiety.

As a Professor of Psychology, Jean had become interested in Holding Therapy after reading a book on attachment by a social worker called Beverly James. She was struck by how such an intrusive treatment could be used when there appeared to be such a lack of good evidence to support it. Much later, in 2010, she came across an article called "To Have and to Hold" in the *British Journal of Social Work*. This article, by Sudbery, Shardlow and Huntingdon, seemed very much like an attempt to rehabilitate holding therapy in the UK.

The style of the article, so common in peer-reviewed journals, gives the impression of elegance and openness. Right from the start, the authors acknowledge criticism by the British Association of Adoption and Fostering and concede that the treatment is controversial. Perhaps this should be applauded. However, not to have been open about this could have given the impression of a cover-up.

The rest of the article appeared to closely examine the arguments. In fact, it simply disguised the fact that nothing meaningful was said about the therapy. Anybody scanning through it may be left with a feeling of reassurance that things couldn't be that bad because a clever-looking article had been written. The problem was that any sort of close questioning would quite quickly reveal that they had learnt nothing about what was going on.

I then read the article that Jean had written in response "To Have and to Hold". She had twice had to re-write because the lawyers at the journal had got nervous and told her it needed toning down. Her main line of argument was that there were simply too many errors of reasoning in the original article and that it failed to evaluate the practices that were taking place in the programme.

After reading the "To Have and to Hold" article, it would be valid to ask an obvious question. "If the treatment was so bad, why did so many of the children fail to describe it that way to the researchers?" To answer this point, Jean responded that this was like saying that the positive words spoken by prisoners of war or the followers of cults justified any ill treatment they may have suffered. Positive responses have been obtained from individuals so enveloped by their environment that they have been persuaded to, as she phrased it, "literally drink the Kool Aid".

The phrase, I felt was an apt one. It was a reference to the "People's Temple", a cult founded in the 1960's by The "Reverend" James Jones. The cult, which had been apparently founded on the well-meaning principles of inter-racial harmony in San Francisco, had developed into a corrupt vehicle for Jones' political ambitions. Facing prosecution, he took his hundreds of devoted followers to the middle of the South American jungle and built a settlement called Jonestown. When the US government began to investigate the cult, Jones persuaded hundreds of men women and children to drink from a vat of poison in order to achieve salvation. The bodies of mothers and fathers lying down and embracing the children they had just killed was a demonstration of the power of mind control when exercised in an isolated environment.

Within the K. Programme, each Attachment Home was in an isolated rural area and the few family and friends who wanted to visit the children were strongly discouraged from doing so onsite. Education was provided in-house and the therapy was never discussed in the homes. As David described there was a

60

culture of submitting to the authority of the programme. The therapy sessions themselves, which ended only when the children capitulated to the authority of the therapist, seemed to be focused on breaking the children. David spoke about how young and inexperienced staff were often employed in the homes, perhaps because they were more easily moulded. Once, David says, during a garden party, a young member of staff had raised the problem that the therapy wasn't underpinned by any decent research. The response was very to the point – "fit in or fuck off".

This atmosphere was further confirmed by reports from the independent advocates who spoke of the programme as "like a cult" and who described the staff as "injected" with an unquestioning attitude to the therapy. This was strong language to use but one needs only to imagine what it would have been like for a young child with no supportive family to exist in this all-embracing world for what would have seemed like a lifetime.

Another academic who has written extensively about Holding Therapy is Rachael Stryker. Stryker's *The Road to Evergreen*, which she wrote at Cornell University, is based on a large number of interviews with therapists, adoptive parents, adoption agency workers and children. The research was conducted mainly at the Evergreen group of clinics in Colorado but also in Russia. The Russian perspective is provided because a number of adoptees were previously placed in, often very deprived, orphanages in the former Soviet Union.

As well a being a useful introduction to the subject of Holding Therapy, Stryker's book, serves as an excellent guide to the issues and themes that have a connection to the subject. Writing as an anthropologist, she discusses the controversy around the diagnoses of Reactive Attachment Disorder and

61

points out that the diagnosis can be a mechanism for avoiding a discussion of uncomfortable issues that surround the behaviour of highly-damaged children.

In order to illustrate the characteristics of RAD and its associated treatments, Stryker focuses on the neurobiology of formerly institutionalised children and Sir Michael Rutter's work on the Romanian orphans study. Stryker also cites the work of Vivien Prior and Danya Glaser, who conclude that the argument seems to be one between those who encourage evidence-based treatments and those who support treatments with no evidence base. She summarises the evidence-based treatments as those that:

> ...either attempt to enhance care giver sensitivity to infants and children or, in the event that this type of intervention does not work, to change care-givers to ones who can be more sensitive to a child's needs.

Treatments that have no evidence base are said to include the Evergreen model of Holding Therapy.

.

The Internet Campaign

At the beginning of 2011, a couple of months after the end of the first police enquiry, there was still no sign of a survivor from the programme. I wrote a couple of posts on the Invisible England blog on the need to raise awareness of the treatment but there were very few visits to the site. I was careful not to name anybody involved as my intention was not to point the finger at individuals or organisations but to generally let people know that this treatment was being used. Life was going on as normal, I had another job and it was as if the whole thing had just slipped away from sight.

From the beginning it seemed important to try to make the issue real. The whole thing was so strange that the simple act of recording it helped me understand that it wasn't the result of an overactive imagination or suspicious mind. I was trying to put something out there just in case anyone was interested. If it wasn't going to get noticed now, perhaps it would be in a few years' time when people had moved on, left their jobs or had different priorities. As it was, I was writing to myself and a couple of others.

When I met David on Facebook, I felt for the first time that progress was being made. After so searching for so long, I had found somebody who had experienced the programme and had lived in the residential home I had visited. This was a direct line to the therapy rooms - that most private of places where nobody really knew what went on apart from the therapists and the child. Of course people observed but, as David recounted so clearly, the therapy changed when others arrived. The holds were loosened, the shouting stopped, the poking and prodding and the abusive language went away – we can be fairly sure there were no splints on the rare occasions social workers came along.

Although the power of this testimony could not be denied, it was several weeks before I felt able to post it on the blog. First, there was the need to take great care of David's emotional well-being. He was still fragile. His resilience enabled him to live a life fuller than many others but he had gone through a lot and to have such personal things in the public domain would be risky.

I felt sure the time was right after we had talked on the phone. He spoke of his family and the difficulty in making himself understood. I felt that I had a connection with him that I think he felt as well. I'm still not sure why this was. Perhaps it was something to do with having lived in Russia as an expat – the sense of an all powerful state and the feeling of being isolated by the language and culture. Maybe it was my work in Children's Services, constantly evaluating the evidence relating to vulnerable children. Whatever it was the connection was there and he allowed me to publish an anonymous version of the account several weeks after he had sent it to me. The response was immediate. There were supportive comments from psychologists, adoption rights campaigners and members of the general public. Even an ex-teacher of David's wrote to praise him for his courage.

To date there are 10 posts that were written on the blog but his first-hand account of the therapy was by far the most visited and seemed the natural heart of the site. Many people commented on its power and authenticity and although some dismissed it or simply ignored it, there was a consensus that it could not be anything other than genuine.

The post after this contained David's account of his foster placement with S. and although this didn't contain any direct reference to Holding Therapy, I felt it gave the treatment a context. There were so many questions raised in relation to the world in which all this took place that it seemed to fill in some of the gaps. Crucially, it contained information about S's interactions with those surrounding her and the dubious practice of fostering children after you had been their therapist. This was surely a conflict of interest at the very least and the dual role of carer and therapist seemed to me to be irreconcilable.

It appeared from the accounts that S. had fostered or adopted at least nine children simultaneously. It was said that Holding Therapy was never mentioned in the household and that some of the care was harsh. It seems that this environment had many similarities with the programme, with control the dominant theme. David also said that the practice of placing ex-programme children in foster placement with staff members was common. This gives rise to the thought that the circle of control was further reinforced by this. A child who was placed with a staff member could experience this as a continuation of his or her period within the programme and much needed outside influences and ways of thinking could be further delayed. There was also the possibility that the data involving children placed in this way could be further manipulated and, for example, placement breakdown rates could be made to improve. In any case, such practices were highly uncommon, even in the late 1990s, and a programme which provided placements, therapy and education could be harshly criticised if further significant roles were informally assigned to staff members.

Although there was increasing interest in the blog, the number of visits I was receiving seemed to level off after June. During this time I received an e-mail from someone using the name "Fainites". To this day I have no idea what their identity is or even if they are male or female. I simply know now that they contributed to the Wikipedia entry on Holding Therapy.

This absolute requirement for anonymity seemed to sum up the experience of many people who had dared to stick their head above the parapet, especially in the United States. There were many examples of academics and psychologists who had been vilified for raising concerns about HT. These attacks were not simply the bad-tempered fallings outs, so common in academia, but coordinated intimidation and internet identity theft known as "sock puppetry". The academic who seemed to have suffered the most from this hostility was Monica Pignotti, an academic from the University of Florida who had co-written some of the articles on HT that had been published in peer-reviewed journals. She had had to endure personal threats and constant insinuation about her public and private life. She was also one of the campaigners who was sued by the therapist Ronald Federici in 2011.

In July 2011 I felt that it would be useful to record interviews and to post them on the blog. The hope was that the act of listening to a voice might trigger a more immediate reaction than the written account. I arranged to interview three people: David, Jean and an American survivor of the therapy who had given an account of her experiences on the US Search for Survivors website. Her testimony had been specifically referred to in Professor Mercer's *British Journal of Social Work* paper and Jean had written to her to ask if I could record an interview.

The interview with David should have been the most straightforward. I had discussed the whole thing with him before and I knew what I was going to cover. In fact, it turned out to be very difficult indeed. He was anxious and there was a sense in which revisiting these experiences again and again was a kind of torture. This problem was something I encountered when I filmed him: the re-telling of his story became distressing and made it less spontaneouse. In a way, the more often he told his story the further away he moved from it. The best account by far was the first, his written account.

Jean's was the easiest interview as she had clearly done this kind of thing before. She spoke about her attendance at the trial of the killers of Candace Newmaker and how a video, made by the therapists, of the killing had been played to the court. When asked about her response to reading David's first-hand account she responded emphatically that her reaction at the time was "I knew it!" She had always suspected this was what was happening but had previously not had clear evidence.

The interview with E. the American survivor was the least predictable. I had never met this person before and I was going to talk to her about her most personal and traumatic experiences. She lived in the Florida Keys and I needed to look up the international time zone in order to work out the right time to call. When we first spoke she seemed shy and anxious. On the other hand, she wanted to tell her story and I could hear the determination in her voice.

She told me how she had experienced HT when she was very young, aged four or five. Her memory was distant but the images were still clear and vivid. She had experienced therapists holding her down and lying on top of her until she gasped for breath. This took place in a room where other young children were being treated in the same way and happened, she said, daily for hours at a time. She had accessed her records and discussed the issue with her parents who had placed her in the institution (which she named) and there was confirmation on both counts that this had happened.

During the interview I could hear the constant growl of low-flying aircraft, a sound that is never far away in the Florida K. So, through the noise of the aircraft engines, she told me about how she had visited a lawyer in New York to attempt to take legal action against the school. In common with David, she said that he found it difficult to categorise. "He really didn't get it."

A few weeks after recording the interviews I met a young man called Harry who worked as a production assistant on advertising shoots. We went for a drink and I told him about the project. "You need to make a film" he said adamantly when I told him about the difficulties we had in getting the message across. "They need to see it for themselves."

Harry showed me some examples of his work - an advert for a DIY store and a promotional film for the Scottish Tourist Board. He was still young and he relished travelling the country working out of a suitcase. When I met him he had just got back from the Scotland shoot – 14 days of constant work in the Scottish Highlands had left him exhausted.

His work as a production assistant meant that he could do a little bit of everything - operate a camera, edit, act as a producer etc. He hadn't done any of these things as a specialist but would be able to do the basics and that was what mattered. In any case, the most important thing was that that he was interested and understood the concepts. He told me the whole thing reminded him of *One Flew over the Cuckoo's Nest* – just substitute Electro-Convulsive Therapy for Holding Therapy. I could see what he meant. Ken Kesey's book dealt with similar themes of control .

So Harry and I agreed to try to make a documentary. The first thing was to travel down to Somerset to see David. I had an idea that I wanted to film the journey down and record our thoughts as we travelled. Harry hired a video camera from a community television studio and we set off very early one morning, planning to get from Liverpool to Somerset and back in one day.

As we drove down he told me about his efforts to explain Holding Therapy to his friends. "I've explained it to a few people in detail", he said. "The first was completely shocked and thought it was terrible and absurd that this could take place. The second was concerned but wanted evidence about where it was happening. The third listened and seemed interested at first but then switched off. The others just weren't that bothered. They listened but then didn't really ask any more questions. I really thought that they would probe more than they did."

We called David as we approached his home village and he met us at a petrol station, He was jokey from the beginning, gently joshing us for taking so much time and telling us it took him only three hours to get to Lancashire when he last went up there. He drove back to his house in front of us and took us down narrow country lanes to his pretty terraced house in the middle of the village. We went in for a few minutes to meet his family and found that there was a kind of harmony there. His wife was shy but welcoming and his children bounded down the stairs, showing us their toys and offering to get some more.

We had a discussion in the street about where to do the interview and decided to drive up to a high point overlooking the village and a place secluded enough for us not to be interrupted. Harry sat in the back, filming us while David drove and smoked. He told us about how he and his partner had become fed up with Lancashire and moved to Somerset. One of the reasons they had moved was because S. had bought them a house there. In fact, it turned out that she hadn't actually bought it for them. She had paid for it and then rented it to them, firstly at a reasonable price and then after the children were born, she doubled the rent. She knew they couldn't afford it and they had to move out. There seemed still to be a need for control even there.

They rented another place and started to thrive. The kids did well and started attending the local primary school. They got on well with the community and were seen as a strong, loving family. Although they continued to see S, this didn't last for long.

When we got to the top of the hill, we found that it was too windy to film. The microphone was able to pick up only the buffeting of what seemed like gale force gusts and we retreated into the hollows that had been dug out in an old quarry mine and filmed an interview that, although powerful, didn not match the immediacy and power of the written account. The video interview was, and could only ever have been, a supplement to the original version. It simply made the connection between how David appeared visually and what he had said and written before.

After the interview we ate in a local restaurant and the waitress gently teased him about his fear of vegetarian food.

He lived on the same road but had never had a meal there before. To their amazement he ordered a vegetarian pasta dish and, even more surprisingly, managed to finish it. While we were eating, Harry turned on his laptop and we checked the statistics for the blog. A normal day now consisted of about 20 hits but today the scale of the graph had changed and the figures on the left-hand side measured the hits in their thousands. The figures for that day only stood at over 3000, with many of the links to source materials having been used. I felt this couldn't be right.

Many of the hits seemed to have come through Twitter and related sites. David tracked back through the links and, after a few minutes said "Who's Ben Goldacre? It took a while to make the link but at that point I knew why there had been so much traffic. I had read Goldacre's book *Bad Science* a year before and I had constantly seen in the kiosks of train stations and promoted by *The Times*. Harry had heard of him as well, through his *Guardian* column. If Goldacre was involved, then that could lead to a lot of publicity. We traced it back and found that he had Tweeted "Blimey, I didn't realise Holding Therapy had come to the UK.. Warning, disturbing accounts if you read around the subject." There was a link to the blog. The tweet had been re-tweeted many times and the messages had spread to Facebook and other messaging services.

There was real significance to Goldacre becoming interested in the topic. He was the son of Michael Goldacre, Professor of Public Health at Oxford; he had been a research fellow at the Institute of Psychiatry, Kings College London and was now research fellow at Nuffield College Oxford. Just as important was his Bad Science column in the *Guardian* and the popular road shows he did with Simon Singh and Brian Cox.

For a few days we felt that things were really moving now and, if there was anything to worry about it was the intrusion that came from too much publicity. We were wrong of course. Twitter can truly be a powerful tool in spreading the word to great numbers of people. It is, however, ephemeral and the hits sloped as steeply downwards as they had risen. Three thousand plus one day then a thousand the next then several hundred until they reached a plateau of twenty to thirty a day. He tweeted again a week or two later and asked if any journalists would be willing to write a story. We got several thousand more hits but nobody was really willing to do the article. Perhaps it was a subject that was too new, too difficult to categorise...perhaps too disturbing.

As we drove back, Harry spoke about his impressions of David. I filmed him talking about how David was so clearly well liked in the village and how he had such an easy sense of humour and how relaxed and apparently well-adjusted his kids were. As we neared home we started to become very tired - we had driven for seven or eight hours that day. We talked about details like the framing of the interview and the problems with sound that we had had. Harry started to become quiet and I could see that he was struggling with his thoughts.

Harry's dispondency came at a bad time. Jean Mercer had managed to arrange for us to interview Professor Edzard Ernst at Exeter University. This was a real coup because, as well as being the first professor of complementary medicine in the world, he had regularly written for the Guardian and was internationally known.

As the date of the interview approached I tried to encourage Harry but I think he just felt that he had given everything and could do no more. He rang me the day before we were due to drive down to Exeter and said that he had been offered a job filming the Olympics. He had to leave immediately to deal with the long preparations and said he was sorry but he wouldn't be able to do the interview. I couldn't believe it, it was the only day Ernst could do and I had no camera or any idea how to operate one if I did.

Harry helped as much as he could. He had booked a professional cameraman in Exeter and got a big discount. It was still expensive but at least it was set up. I took the train down and met the owner of a local film production company. When we drove up together to the Peninsula Medical School I was struck by how out of the way it seemed. There were a number of twists and turns through what looked like an industrial estate until we arrived at what was clearly a modern university building. His secretary came to meet us in reception and helped us carry our film equipment through to his department. As we walked down these winding corridors I heard an academic remark sarcastically "filming are we?" It was a sign of the tensions that had existed at the university ever since Ernst had gone public with his criticism of the homeopathic remedies promoted by the Duchy of Cornwall.

Ernst was known for his practice of applying rigorous scientific tests to complimentary medicines and, in relation to this, had called Prince Charles a "snake oil salesman". This, in Exeter, I suppose was tantamount to heresy and the Vice Chancellor had become involved in the controversy. The upshot of this was that Ernst was accused of breaking confidentiality in relation to a study that he had been working on and, although he was eventually cleared, he had suffered the indignity of a highly unpleasant investigation and was, for a time, considered persona non grata by the University hierarchy.

By the time we had come to see him his reputation had been restored and he had continued to enjoy success through, among other things, a book with Simon Singh on Chiropractors called *Trick or Treatment*. Singh had recently been sued by the Association of Chiropractors for writing a

Guardian article on the subject and, after a protracted court case and appeal had been cleared of libel. The case had brought home to me the extent to which powerful interests could use the libel laws in the UK to intimidate individuals who speak out about unproven and dangerous treatments. Ben Goldacre had been subjected to the same treatment by an Austrian billionaire when he raised concerns about the lack of efficacy of homeopathic remedies produced by his company.

Professor Ernst's reserved and courteous secretary asked us to wait for him until he was ready to see us. When he opened his door he invited us in and asked about the framework of the interview and what it would be used for. He had already had some information from Professor Mercer and he had agreed to see me on her recommendation.

The pitfalls of this kind of interview must have been apparent to him as he had had experiences with the media in the past. He asked where the interview would be shown and then settled down into the process as Rick set up his equipment. I asked if he could provide longer answers without waiting for further questions as we would be editing my voice but, in the event he didn't need the guidance. He spoke eloquently and to the point about the key issues and at the end we felt that a significant event had occurred. A world-class scientist had unequivocally condemned the use of Holding Therapy in the UK. He had taken a risk and spoken about the use of large amounts of public money for an unproven, expensive and dangerous treatment that simply "frightens children" in an attempt to "break them as human beings". He referred to Ofsted's inaction and lack of scrutiny, said that he felt that the public had "no notion that these practices are taking place". He recommended that "informing the public is the only way of moving this issue forward".

The film went on the blog and the following day the police got involved again. I found out the news from David. He told me that Detective Inspector C. had been on the phone to him. He had told him that he had asked for him by name and said that he knew he was the person who had written the first-hand account on the blog. David asked him where he had got his number from. The inspector told him he got it from the K. programme. He had gone to them asking if they had any idea who it was and they had said they thought it was David. Perhaps they had recognised his voice on the audio recording.

"Somebody's made a complaint," he said. Apparently it had been initiated by the blog. "It's quite impressive isn't it?", he said. "Whoever's writing it feels very passionately about it, don't they? Sound like somebody I know (pause)." Somebody like..." and at that point he said my name. David didn't say anything but laughed He hadn't said a word to confirm or deny the truth of this but it was no less of a confirmation than if he had written a letter to tell the inspector that it was me. I felt angry with the inspector about this as I felt that he had manoeuvred David into an indiscretion

I waited two days after this and then pulled the blog. I consulted David beforehand but it didn't make him any happier. He had seen the blog as something that described part of his life, in a way that had not been expressed fully before. So, with the single press of a button, a part of him had disappeared. It was sudden and he was quite understandably upset about it.

On my part I had been worried what the Inspector would do next. He could, I knew, have simply picked up a phone and found out where I worked. He could then have made a call with the pretext of collecting information and then mentioned, in passing that I was involved. The result for me would have been an effective dismissal. Of course there would have been a short delay but that would have been all. The prospects of getting another job would have been slim as my potential employers are, on one level or another, interconnected. The mortgage would not have been paid, pressure would have been put on my family life and the children would have suffered. It was all too predictable and for all the pain I caused David I couldn't keep the blog going.

Following this, David was told to visit his local police station where he would be interviewed. The PC who did this appeared confused by a lot of the material. "It's not good, is it?" she said, eventually. "No, it's not," said David firmly.

The police had finally launched a criminal investigation and, after making initial enquiries had found enough to be seriously concerned about. They wrote to David saying that they intended to collect evidence which they would present to the Crown Prosecution Service. The prosecutors would then decide whether there was a case worthy of prosecution.

The second good thing to come out of it was that we heard that S. had been suspended. For a long time David had been in e-mail contact with a manager of one of the K Attachment Homes. She seemed to be in the oddly conflicted situation of continuing to work for the organisation but providing us with inside information and even encouraging us in our efforts to get this out in the open. As with so many others, her feelings of horror about the practices seemed to inhabit her unconscious and she seemed free to take only certain actions to deal with it and unable or unwilling to behave more proactively – she could cheer us on form the sidelines but couldn't leave the company.

It was a theme that came up again and again, people could do what they could and then they couldn't do anything more. Markers were put down in the sand and then left alone.

Actually this didn't really matter. The BAAF statement, the BJSW article, the journey to see David, the blog and the interview with Ernst. These collective efforts of the well-intentioned would hopefully amount to something that might make a difference in the future.

The knowledge that S. had been suspended was good news but didn't mean that she had admitted culpability or that she would face any disciplinary action. It simply meant that they had done the usual thing and asked her to stay away from work while they did whatever they needed to do. Actually, because she was a freelance consultant now it's debatable whether it was even an official suspension. They had simply stopped using her services for a short period.

The insider also told us that K. programme employees had all been instructed not to contact any of the programme's former residents. This wasn't a surprise but was diametrically opposed to previous K programme practices. In the past, strong links seem to have been kept up between the young people and staff members after they had left the programme. Indeed many of the children seemed to have been fostered by the staff. How this got past Children's Services is difficult to understand. Perhaps it came from the need to avoid secure accommodation at all costs. You can imagine how pressured and well-meaning social workers couldn't face the prospect of multiple placement breakdowns. They cut corners and didn't follow protocols but they wouldn't have been the first to do so.

Yet, in spite of all the excuses, there is no getting away from the fact that this was a highly systematic programme. The whole intricate structure was almost completely self-contained which should have rung alarm bells from the very beginning. The right questions were not asked and the gaps were all glossed over. A psychotherapist with the gift of the gab managed to bend the rules so much, over so many years, that the final result left some concerned individuals scratching their heads and wondering how it had all came about. It also left some very well-respected people wonderering how on earth they found themselves involved in all this.

The insider at the K programme must also have wondered how she managed to find herself in such a bizarre situation. She had probably applied for the job through her desire to help vulnerable children. There was probably little discussion of the therapy among the staff or young people and they probably found consolation in the fact that there had been "studies" undertaken or that there were "independent" professionals involved. Even now, when she knew what was going on, she couldn't bring herself to take decisive action.

She did, however, know that she wanted it to stop. When she found out that David was taking a stand there was something inside her that wanted to do everything in her power to help him tell his story. She wrote him an e-mail in late 2011, just after the police began their criminal investigation:

> You told it how it was. I'll only say it one more time but… you was a little boy hun and no one listened to you. Now you're a man and they have to take notice.

Analysis

It is important to establish what is now known about the K programme. It is not in question that there is a programme of Holding Therapy that treats children in the 11 associated residential children's homes. It is also undisputed that the therapy itself takes place in one location, at the N. Business Park and that each of the children experiences HT on a weekly basis for no less than two years. We know the dates when the company was founded (1995) because this is registered at Companies House. We know that there are approximately 40 children treated within the programme at any one time because the 14 year contract with the independent advocacy contract was exclusively for these children and these are the figures recorded by the advocates. We know that Holding Therapy, of the kind described by BAAF Position Statement 4, is used at the homes because the Sudberry et al article acknowledges it is.

We have evidence that the Holding Therapy used is of a form that is highly intrusive because the company's own literature is open about this. We have evidence that relates very specifically to the kind of techniques used because in August 2010, the Managing Director of the K. stated to me that the process described in a chapter of a book called *The Extra Dimension* by S. was an accurate description of contemporary therapeutic practice at the K Attachment Homes. This chapter describes a step-by-step guide to therapeutic practice, it states that it may be necessary to "deliberately distress the child" and it is a document that was supplied by K. to the advocacy organisation.

The question then arises as to David's experiences. First it needs to be asked how sure we can we be that he is telling the truth and that his descriptions are an accurate account of the therapy. If we agree that he is completely accurate and honest then we need to consider whether his experiences were unique or whether we should consider that many, if not all, the other children went through similar experiences.

So let us consider the first question. Is he telling the truth? My first reaction to this question is that everyone who has expressed a view on his written "first-hand account" appears to be in no doubt that his description is genuine. While the overwhelming majority express admiration for his courage and condemn the perpetrators of these practices, there are a few who are indifferent to his description and others who feel that these were terrible actions but that the events were historical and irrelevant to current practices. They express these things but I have never heard anyone say simply that they don't believe him. It seems that the immediacy of his descriptions and the coherence of the narrative gel in such a way that it is almost futile to doubt him. It is also the case that his Social Services records produce, with his account, a watertight argument.

Then there are the more challenging questions. Did his contemporaries at K experience the same verbally and physically abusive treatment? Did all the children in the late nineties experience the poking, prodding, pinning down, verbal abuse and taunting? David says they did and one would have to ask why he would lie about this. One also has to ask, if they did it to David why would they stop at him, especially if the literature produced by them at the time seemed to justify this kind of practice? What we can say is that there was nothing in place to prevent it from happening to all the children. David's social worker claims now (I have seen the e-mails) that she had no idea of the nature of the treatment he was going through. In any case, David has been in touch with a few former residents and a current manager of one of the homes and they have confirmed that others went through similar things at the time.

The question of whether David's contemporaries experienced similar things and whether the residents still do now can, in some ways, be illuminated by my own evidence. Although I am the author of this book I am also a protagonist in the story. My role at the advocacy organisation enabled me to speak to all the advocates at length, receive regular monthly reports from all the homes and access to records. I also was able to visit one of the homes and to have a lengthy one-to-one discussion with the Managing Director. On the basis of all this information, I discussed my concerns with the assistant head of the legal department, informed all middle and senior mangers and lawyers and stated to the Chief Executive that I felt that the only course of action was to inform the police. The records, the advocates and the Managing Director's account left me in very little doubt that most, if not all, of the children within the programme continued to experience highly intrusive and abusive treatment.

Another key argument that counters the view that the abusive treatment was historical and not relevant to the current programme is the fact that S remains the sole trainer of all the therapists. She was the co-founder of the company and until recently continued to be an employee. She continues to be employed as a consultant and is pictured on the website in two promotional videos – in one demonstrating the use of Holding Therapy and, in another, speaking on the same platform as the Children's Commissioner for Northern Ireland at the opening of the parent company's new headquarters.

To use the argument that it was all historical and therefore irrelevant is the equivalent of saying that a person who abused a child a number of years ago should be entrusted to work, in private, with the most vulnerable children in society. However, there is overwhelming evidence that the highly intrusive and aggressive treatment continues to be used.

Once we have addressed whether the treatment was and continues to be abusive, it is necessary to consider the checks and balances that were, or should have been, in place. The children are said to be mainly Looked After, that is, they are children within the care system. They were placed by local authorities, who had at least shared parental responsibility for them, and as a consequence of this it was necessary for these local authorities to give informed consent to any treatment that was used. A second mechanism to safeguard the children was the inspection regime enforced by Ofsted. Ofsted had taken over a few years earlier from the Commission for Social Care Inspectorate. The other key safeguard was the Independent Advocacy Service that I worked for as an Operations Manager.

Let us consider these institutions one at a time. The social workers and managers who work for local authorities have a duty to be fully aware of any treatment the children undergo during their placement. It is especially true that they should have knowledge of highly intrusive and controversial treatments and it is evident that the peer-reviewed literature in the USA, the BAAF Position Statement and the Sudbery et al paper make it clear at the very least that Holding Therapy is highly controversial. Some of the evidence demonstrating that the local authorities didn't know about the nature of the treatment comes from David's Social Worker and her manager. They have apparently said that they had no idea that it was intrusive or controversial. It was also the case that an advocate was reprimanded for informing a child's social worker about the nature of the treatment – which implies that the social worker did not already know. If they didn't know about the treatment they can't have given informed consent, and therefore the children were assaulted. On the other hand, if they did know about the treatment, they were responsible for asking further questions about its efficacy.

In relation to Ofsted, there is clear evidence that this body, responsible for inspecting both the homes and the therapy, has not fulfilled its duties. The 2009 report into the K Attachment Centre at Rossendale does not mention the words Holding Therapy or Attachment Therapy in any way. If one reads the report without any prior knowledge of the fact that holding therapy is used at K programme, there would be no indication that any form of touching is employed at all, let alone planned restraint, coercion and deliberate provocation. This, for me, is one of the most remarkable omissions in the whole affair. The first question that was asked by Detective Superintendent C. was in relation to the governance of the therapy. The Managing Director said to me that Ofsted was responsible for this. Detective Inspector C, after his first inquiry, said that there was no governance. Whatever the truth of it, it is clear that there was no *effective* governance relating to the programme.

Finally, what of the independent advocacy supposedly provided by the organisation I worked for? This was a vital part of the jigsaw, as the first things that would be wheeled out when any questions were asked were the Salford University study and the fact that independent advocates were representing the wishes and feelings of the children – ammunition to shut up the most vocal critics. Yet, as I have described, out of the four current advocates, one (10 years at K) described the organisation as a cult in which none of the children ever gave informed consent to a treatment of which he had only a vague knowledge. The second (three years at K) said she thought the treatment was talking therapy. The third (two years at K) said that she vaguely knew there was some controversy but had never asked further questions. The fourth had asked more searching questions but had not raised the issue with me for the 10 months I had worked as her manager.

There were many good advocates working at the charity – teachers, social workers, lawyers, youth workers but only one had ever thought to ask the children what was happening to them every week, year after year. Even the one who had initially questioned things failed to speak up again for many months.

We now move on the question of wider responsibility. The organisations directly responsible for the safety and well-being of these hundreds of children and the millions of pounds of public money clearly failed. However, it was not only these people who knew about the programme. Over the years, lawyers, academics and police officers have known about the K programme. They knew something of concern was going on and some of them, frankly, were wondering when it was all going to come out. Robin Tolson QC who was initially consulted by David's solicitors had heard of the practice and gave the impression that he felt it was merely a matter of time before a case came to light.

Perhaps the most significant reason why nothing was done about the programme is because of all the vested interests involved in keeping quiet about it. It seems clear that the practice has taken hold in the UK almost by accident. Some eminent people such as Tinbergen supported it in the early days and then it became useful or convenient for certain organisations to continue using it, writing in support of it or marketing it. From that point on, it could be argued that anyone who came into contact with the programme colluded with the whole thing because they did nothing about it. It became buried in the back of their minds and was just too uncomfortable to address.

Another aspect of accountability concerns citizens who live near to where the treatment is conducted, and indeed close to where the children live and are educated. This includes the residents of Rossendale, who include the local Conservative MP who lives a few miles from what is probably one of the largest programmes of Holding Therapy in the world. The interesting question for me is how much these residents know about the programme. Even if they have heard of it, do they really know the details and have they asked the proper questions?

In any account of a human rights abuse the question always arises as to why the issue has emerged at the particular time, sometimes decades after the initial events took place. To illustrate this point it may be useful to examine large-scale abuses that have taken place in this century and the last. Professor of Philosophy at MIT and political activist Noam Chomsky often discusses the question of power relationships and their influence on current political discourse. He asks for example, why there was little reporting of the East Timor massacres in Indonesia when hundreds of thousands of, mainly landless peasants, were killed by the Suharto regime. The answer, Chomsky argues, lies in the need for the US to consider its own strategic interests and the economic opportunities that became available for US corporations. In contrast, there is no shortage, quite rightly, of information and discussion in relation to the Gulag that operated in Soviet Russia. The archives remain preserved in museums, film footage is ingrained in public consciousness and memoirists and activists are awarded Nobel prizes.

Anne Applebaum's *GULAG* is a masterpiece of historical narrative but it is important to consider the circumstances which allowed it to be written. Appelbaum's work describes, in devastating fashion, the numbers, the geography, the individual lives and considers the political background to the camps but there are considerable vested interests in her documenting the atrocities. The collapse of the Soviet Union and the emerging independence of former Soviet states means that convincingly described historical narratives have great bearing on contemporary politics in the region. It is not wrong that this should be this case but it is useful to know that powerful interests stand to gain from these stories being told.

In contrast, who stands to gain from the story of the K Programme being told? The only individuals who will gain directly are the children who went through the two years of therapy. It is only they who will then have the opportunity to make sense of what happened to them in the name of treatment and then gradually they may be able to rebuild their lives. The difficulty is that these former residents are, by definition, the most vulnerable members of our society. That is precisely why their local authorities took it upon themselves to exercise parental responsibility on their behalf. They don't have articulate parents who can lobby their local MPs or get together with other parents to form a pressure group. The options open to the parents of children who had their organs removed by Alder Hey Hospital, or the parents of the children who died at Bristol Hospital as a result of incompetent heart surgery, are not open to the former residents of K. Attachment Homes.

The barrier in front of these former residents is formidable. Firstly, they were vulnerable when they entered the programme. There were no family members identified as able to care for them and there may have been a number of foster placement moves or adoption breakdowns beforehand. Secondly, the programme consisted of isolating them from mainstream society – education was later provided by the organisation itself. Every week for two years they underwent the therapy, where they were deliberately provoked and restrained until they broke down and complied. Every other young person they came into contact with underwent the same treatment. There was no publicity about the programme and most psychologists and mainstream therapists were not aware of it so there was no context around which they can describe the treatment to other professionals or within the community. Every aspect of this situation acted against a survivor speaking out effectively and taking restorative action. In fact, given these circumstances, it is remarkable that a survivor has managed to give his account of the therapy so vividly and fully.

Beyond all this, there is a final observation that seems to remove further doubts that this programme is in every way a sham. The early use of holding/attachment therapy on children diagnosed with autism and within the programmes in the Evergreen area of Colorado is predicated on the theory that the children were being encouraged to attach to their care giver. This could be their adoptive parent, their biological parent or a foster carer. The principles behind this are unsubstantiated but, even if one were to suspend disbelief for a moment and accept this theory, it can be seen that the programme cannot be justified even in its own terms. For the question remains, who are the children meant to be attaching to? The therapists?

The K programme is unique in that the adoptive parent or the foster carer is generally absent. The therapist is an individual who treats the child intermittently and then withdraws. The residential workers who are present are generally shift workers who have a temporary relationship with the child. This simple observation sheds light on the fact that the function of the programme is not primarily to help children to attach but to make them more compliant. If this is accepted, an uncomfortable truth becomes apparent - whoever the programme exists for, it doesn't seem to exist for the benefit of vulnerable children.

Appendix 1

Invisible England Blog Posts

Never Let Me Go – Raising Awareness of Holding Therapy in the UK

Are you aware of Holding Therapy? If not, I wouldn't be surprised, many social workers psychiatrists and psychologists are not either. This is despite the fact that substantial amounts of public money have been spent on it over the last decade in the UK. Holding Therapy is a highly intrusive therapy which is used with some of the most vulnerable children in the country. Originally developed in the USA, particularly around the area of Evergreen in Colorado, it involves the holding of a child in a lying position by two therapists. A description of this practice can be found in Wikipedia (Holding Therapy is also known as Attachment Therapy).

In 2006 the British Association of Adoption and Fostering issued an extensive position statement that highlighted the fact that Attachment Therapy is "neither justifiable or effective". It states that the nature of the therapy "effectively makes it impossible to withdraw consent". The statement also contains a final paragraph headed "The dangers of institutional abuse of children". The British Journal of Social Work has recently published an article attempting to rehabilitate the practice and an article will shortly be published in the journal in response to this. This blog will later provide more information on the history, politics and economics of Holding Therapy but, in the meantime, it may be helpful to look at the information available through the links (Wikipedia is a good place to start).

This is a call for people in the UK to find out more about Holding Therapy. As UK taxpayers we are funding this highly controversial practice and, as responsible citizens, I feel we are responsible for understanding what is being done to our most vulnerable children.

Why is it Important to Raise Awareness of Holding Therapy in the UK?

How widespread is Holding Therapy in England? At present there is only one programme that we are aware of in England. This consists of 10 or 11 small children's homes owned by a private company. The children are aged from 8-18 and are taken to a single therapy centre on a weekly basis. This therapy is similar to the therapy described in the BAAF 2006 Position statement and continues for no less than two years for each child. Almost all the children are in care and are funded by local authorities.

For me, the starting point is how such a substantial programme of Holding Therapy can exist when a major organisation such as the BAAF has effectively called for it to be banned?. There have been no clinical trails proving its efficacy and there is no meaningful governance that oversees its practice. The question that I feel needs to be asked is why are local authorities placing their most vulnerable children in these places if there is no scientific evidence to prove that the treatment works?

One explanation could be that these local authorities may not be aware of the BAAF statement, that HT is not proven or they may not even be actively aware that the therapy they have commissioned is not simply talking therapy. If this is true, and they are not aware of the nature of the therapy, then (as they exercise PR) they have not legally given consent to a highly intrusive practice and it could therefore be argued that the children are being assaulted.

So why make such an issue of HT? The reason, I feel, lies in the nature of the therapy itself. There are certain aspects of it which ring alarm bells. There are features such as the "strong encouragement" of eye contact and the potential need to "deliberately distress" the child before they eventually break down and capitulate that has echoes of the way high-demand groups (cults) operate. A response that is sometimes heard in relation to HT is that "it works". The question for me is, for who? The danger surely is that such a prolonged and intensive programme such as this may work well to create short-term compliance but may lead to serious long-term problems which have not been fully considered.

At worst, it could be argued that the practice of HT could sometimes be taking away an aspect of a child's humanity, the ability to respond independently and critically to their environment . In other words, it is a version of the Clockwork Orange debate – the merits of state-sponsored brainwashing of children and young people. The wider question is why has society allowed this practice to continue in the UK for so long (14 years in relation to this programme)? There has been no significant public debate but some professionals and members of the public have heard something of the practice. Why have they not investigated further? Why weren't further questions asked? It is what this tells us about the society that we live in that raises the really important issues.

A First-Hand Account of Holding Therapy in the UK

As far as I am aware this is the first time a first-hand account of Holding Therapy in the UK has been published on the internet. I have seen and heard evidence from a number of sources that reassures me that this description is genuine. This child would have experienced this treatment on a regular basis between the ages of 11 and 13 and the sessions sometimes could last for several hours, usually only ending when the child submitted to the authority of the therapists. Holding Therapy will probably have taken place today with a number of different children, sometimes as young as 8.

The Therapy sessions them selves were quite traumatic

One other adult usally one of the unit residential staff had to lie down feet on the one adult who would then hold the feet down on the top half one hand behind the therapist back been held by the person sat next to her one hand place on my chest held down my the therapist and constant forced eye to eye contant if i looked way my head would have been pinned in the direction of the therapist and if i tried to say no another hand would firmly clasped over my mouth which would send me into a fit of rage all this was also backed up with alot of shouting and swearing the therapist would say things like is this what your fucking birth mum did to you did she and the hand would come of my mouth for a responce this seemed to go on for ages in the end i was so drained and broken and scared i just said yes in therapy i was constanly prevented from rubbing my eye if i had an itch prevented from stretching prevented from doing all nataural that i human being does to relive a discomfort and sureley that is taking away a basic human right but at the end of each session broken tired it was

93

kind of drilled in that all this was ok and they always managed to manipulate you to feeling ok when you left the session. another time i was wrapped in a blankett pind down and held so tight all i could feel was fright so i responded again with agression looking back this is what they wanted break you down to comply. i also attented so called intensive therapy where there would be 2 therapist again pinned down basicly given torrents of abuse poked proded until i reached agression again. I was i liveley lad growing up always trying to push boundries but during my time at ..... turned into this agressive monster attacked so many staff bit them punched them hit i had many bruises from this place and sometimes looked quite ill and run down i kept getting told they would help me but infact it was there methods that were turning me into somthing else in one instance i had splints put on my arms to imobilise me then they woud start laughing at amd humiliating me and again i went into a rage put power less as i was splinted in the end my violence got so out of contol i as kicking off every day staff were hospitalised in the end it was decided .....couldnt meet my needs due to the increase in violent behaviour which now but that is what they turned me into after meeting and meeting its was decided i should go into a secure unit but then at the last second ..... said i want to foster this boy my therapist and director of fostering well that is a different story for years in the placement with them was ruled by fear and attachment therapy was never mentioned in her home she would bring kids back from work and make them sleep on the stairs on the floor and make them look after her disabled son who would often beat them up just to make them apprciate there own home this therapy is not about helping children its about making a child love or attach through fear! i tried to tell my head teacher in the late 90's about what was going on she seemed concerned but again ..... and ..... got away with it and i got the biggest bollocking of my life. as for the staff in the units them selves were taken young carers with no experience

94

been manipulated to work the ..... way alot have staff have left as they felt this was wrong and one member of staff in my defence reported the dog bone incident and also reported doctoring of ..... logs to put ..... in a better light which i have in .....whilst in the care of.....and ..... to my knolledge never had an inderpendent evaluation until i was 14 when i went to the ..... with ..... to be assed which was not inderpendent as the doctor was a freind of .....once these people have these children in there care its kept very close to ..... the ouside world was totally oblivious to what was going on in my mind as social workers didnt understand the practices now i am left with anixety and never 100% trust anyone i am rid with guilt i feel stupid as i said am trying another therapy through the NHS to fix all the crap ..... and ..... did to me

i hope this is ok for starters if there is any direct question you wish to ask please do so as i do seem to rambble on some what

11 Responses to *A First-hand Account of Holding Therapy in the UK*

Jean Mercer

April 5, 2011 at 9:29 pm

Thanks so much for telling this part of your story. Many survivors of holding therapy are too intimidated and anxious to let the public know their experiences, but it's only through individual bravery like what's shown here that we can be sure to put a stop to cruel and inappropriate treatment masquerading as psychological intervention.

Von

April 6, 2011 at 2:44 am

You've done a great job of explaining how it was so that all can understand the abuse of holding therapy.Thank you.

Sunday

April 6, 2011 at 5:04 am

I found your blog through Jean Mercer, thank you for getting this kind of therapy and it's destructive techniques out in the open. I just recently have gotten to the point where I can talk about my similar experiences from my youth. Hopefully the more people who speak out the more likely that this dark chapter of child therapy will come to a close.

Fainites

April 6, 2011 at 9:56 am

Well done for exposing this. I admire your courage.

Monica Pignotti, PhD

April 7, 2011 at 9:13 pm

Thank you for having the courage to come forward and blow the whistle on this abuse in the name of "therapy". The more people who do this, the more the mental health establishment is going to have no choice but to take these complaints seriously. Shame on the profession and on licensing boards for looking the other way in many different countries.

Daisy

April 12, 2011 at 1:27 am

Thank you for sharing your experiences of HT. I heard about it when I lived in Manchester in the 80/90's but I was confused about it.

I worked in the residential care system in the 90s and although I didn't witness anything like what you went through but I agree that children and young people were sometimes negelected and abused by those who were suppose to be protecting and caring for them. I left in the end after challenging many things but because I could not bear to a part of it anymore and even unit managers were not listened to by those with the power to make a difference. A Senior manager, with overall responsibility for all of the residential units inthe area, would visit from time to time and she really was completely out of touch and uninterested – she would chat on about her own children, their many talents and how they loved snowboarding. Insensitive and self important!

During my time there, one girl was raped (not within the home but by an older person that she knew). A senior member of staff told me she did not believe the girl – she said she had spoken with one of the police officers investigatin who had said she could tell when a victim was lying. I challenged this and was listened to but only because i had previous experience working with rape victims. In fact the girl's own account was wholly credible and there was no reason at all to doubt her – she was in a state of trauma and that was clear to everyone.

I have heard countless stories of abusive foster care and I witnessed so much indifference within the residential system (specifically within the social services higher management, the police and some health professionals). I was lucky in that I had two managers who were very committed to young people but it was almost impossible to challenge the system. The young people had no voice and not power over there own lives. It was even worse in the private sector. Often people do not disclose such things until later in adulthood, so many of those stories have yet to come out.

Your story is very important and you tell it with an emotional intelligence that is very powerful. Good for you for speaking out and for telling the truth of what happened to you. I can ony imagine how horrific your experiences were – they need to be heard because most people have no idea that these things went on – do they still go on?

Above all I that hope that you get the support and the healing that you so much deserve.

warmest wishes to you

anonymous

It was a good thing you survived. be strong and don't be afraid to get back on those who have hurt you. show them that you were not intimidated with what they did to you. show them that you are stronger than them and they can never let you down. stay strong and carry on with life!

A

Your story is incredible..I can't say how much I admire you....I´m from Czech republic and I do some translating for an organization which is trying to stop this "Holding epidemy" in my country...and I have one question..what are the dots in your story for...I´m affraid, that my knowledge of english is not that great yet, and because I would like to translate your story properly, co it can be understood poperly, I need to know that. Would you please explain it to me?
And once again...you are very brave, and thank you very much for exposing this dark part of your life to us, hope it will help to stop this crazy conduct.

anyachaika

A.

Thank you for your comments. The dots are in place of the names of the therapist and the organisation that conduct this therapy.

It would be great if this account could be publicised in your country

Reply

Rose

August 23, 2011 at 5:05 pm

Incredible guts – every good wish for a happy future for you

Reply

faith

September 8, 2011 at 12:07 pm

You are so Brave! who ever these people need to be brought to some sort of justice

The Origins of Holding Therapy in the UK

When all the information is assessed and one takes a step back, it is astonishing how systematic and audacious the (sole) programme of Holding Therapy in the UK is. It is useful just to highlight the main features of the project. The forty children within the programme at any one time seem to be mainly subject to Care Orders or Interim Care Orders. This means that they will have been through the court process and been subject to multi-professional meetings involving social workers, teachers, health professionals etc. They will have been represented by solicitors, barristers and Guardian ad Litems and had expert reports written about them by psychologists and psychiatrists. Their current placements will have been paid for by tri-partite funding from health, education and social care and, at a conservative estimate, cost the taxpayer several thousand pounds a week per placement. This means that it is entirely possible that millions of pounds of public money has been spent on a highly-intrusive treatment on our most vulnerable children which few people have heard of. Faced with such a situation, it may be helpful to look at the origins of Holding Therapy in the US and in the UK.

Holding Therapy in the US generally has its foundations in Robert Zaslow's rage-reduction therapy in the 60s and 70s and psychoanalytic theories of rage reduction. The therapy was frequently used in a number of clinics around the Evergreen area of Coloradoafter Foster Cline founded his first clinic there in the 70s and was, in its early stages, used as a treatment for autistic children. The practice was later used as a treatment for Reactive Attachment Disorder and, following the collapse of the Soviet Union, frequently used with Russian and other Eastern European children who often had been raised in orphanages and adopted by parents in the US.

In the UK it seems that a key event in the introduction of Holding Therapy was a visit by the American psychologist Martha Welch in the 80s. Welch had written a book called Holding Time which advocates the use of HT on autistic children, she later adapted the treatment for children diagnosed with RAD. It appears that, during this visit she was initially supported by a number of influential academics, notably Nikolaas Tinbergen and his wife Elisabeth, My understanding is that a small number of clinics started using HT as a treatment for autism at this time but these gradually ceased to operate as the theory that autism was caused by attachment failures with the mother was discredited. A small number of HT therapists also started to use the treatment on children diagnosed with Reactive Attachment Disorder but these also soon started to reduce in number particularly, it seems, after the publication of the British Association of Adoption and Fostering Position Statement (4) which effectively called for the treatment to be banned.

By far the largest, most systematic and sophisticated programme of Holding Therapy in the UK began in about 1996 and was started in the North of England by a foster carer and her social worker. The programme began as a non-profit making project but was soon reinvented into a private company. One of the founders who for many years was the head of therapy is now a consultant employed by the company. It has been reported that she remains the only trainer of therapists the company has ever had. In 2002 this company commissioned a local university to undertake an evaluation of its therapeutic practices. The university website records that it was paid £31,000 to undertake the study which consisted of a number of semi-structured interviews with staff and children. This study was generally positive but vague in terms of the therapy itself – it reported only a few negative "outlier responses".

Following the commissioning of this report in 2002/3, a number of articles appeared in the national press. These appeared to simply reproduce the claims of the company and strikingly failed to question, in any way, the nature of the therapy. There was even a feature on the BBC woman's Hour which essentially seemed to advertise the service. However, after 2003 there were significantly fewer items in the media and by 2006 the company seems to have been in significant financial trouble – items in local news papers confirm this. It may not be a coincidence that the highly critical (against AT) BAAF Position Statement 4 appeared around this time.

What happened next is extensively recorded in the financial press and can be researched on the Companies House website. This, still relatively small, company was bought by a much bigger parent company, based outside the country. This may be significant for a number of reasons. It was around this time that a number of concerns were raised around private equity firms buying up small groups of children's homes and foster care companies in, so-called "distressed sale" buyouts. A common theme was that these, sometimes family owned businesses, were being stripped of any elements that did not clearly contribute to profit-making. The effect on this particular company may have been that the owners were much further removed from what was going on and may not have cared about it as long as it didn't affect the balance sheet. Indeed, it has been said that high-level supervision of practice within the homes may have been conducted by the Chief Financial Officer.

There is a theme that runs through the recent history of HT in the UK like the letters in a stick of Brighton Rock. It is simply that the people responsible for ensuring the safety and well-being of these Looked After Children don't seem to have asked any questions – they appear to have simply turned a blind eye. The inspectors responsible for its governance don't even mention the words Holding Therapy or Attachment Therapy, the social workers don't seem to even know, or say they don't know, that this kind of therapy is taking place. In truth, it could have always been said that, as Fainities (a commentator on a previous post) has highlighted, we never really knew the detail of what was going on – academics such as Prior and Glaser presumed it was a nuturing form of HT that was being practised in theUK. It could always be glossed over in this way. This get-out clause is precisely why first-hand accounts of HT, such as the description published on 5th April on this blog, are so vitally important.

A Chronology of Significant Events

1996 - A programme of Holding Therapy, later to become the largest and most systematic in the world, is founded in the North of England by a foster carer and her social worker

2002 - A local university is paid £31,000 to conduct a study of the Holding Therapy within the programme

2006 - The British Association of Adoption and Fostering condemns Attachment/Holding therapy and effectively call for it to be banned in Position Statement 4 (see links)

2006 - An American Professional Society on the Abuse of Children (APSAC) report condemns Holding Therapy

2006 - The company that manages the programme is bought by a much larger (foreign) parent company. The Holding Therapy itself remains restricted to the 11 attachment homes within the original programme

2010 - After 8 years, findings from a university study are published in the British Journal of Social Work

7.9.2011 - The police begin an inquiry into allegations by a professional from an independent agency that the therapy in the programme constitutes abuse, that no meaningful consent is obtained and that the children's human rights are being breached

5.4.2011 - A young man writes his first-hand account of the Holding Therapy he experienced within this programme on a weekly basis between the ages of 11 - 13.

19.4.2011 - The young man obtains legal advice.

1.5.2011 - Professor Jean Mercer publishes her rejoinder to the British Journal of Social Work article, heavily criticising its methods and raising significant concerns about the practice of Holding Therapy.

27.8.2011 (5.47pm)- Ben Goldacre of the Guardian becomes the first mainstream journalist to raise concern and awareness of Holding Therapy in the UK through his Twitter account. He provides a link to Invisible England.

12.9.2011 - Professor Edzard Ernst is interviewed by Invisible England - he describes the Holding Therapy used in the programme as unproven, expensive (public money is used), dangerous and frightening. He states that he feels the only way forward is to inform the public.

2011 - The police interview the survivor of Holding Therapy and begin a criminal investigation into the programme. It is understood that 40 children (almost all Looked After by Local Authorities) continue to be subjected to this treatment on a weekly basis for no less than 2 years.

Appendix 2

Correspondence

Correspondence from Professor David Howe to David Hanson

5th March 2012

David,

I have knowledge of the website that you mention. I have never worked for the organisation in Rawtenstall, although I did visit it once one afternoon, I think round about 2001. I did agree to co-write a paper with S in 2003 to help her describe the work of the K Attachment Centre so that the other people could be aware of the centre's philosopies and practices. This was my only (indirect) contact with the organisation which occurred briefly nearly 10 years.

I am not a therapist. I have never endorsed holding therapy, only described it so that others could get a sense of what was involved. My personal view is that children are most likely to benefit from secure, loving and sensitively attuned relationships with their parents and carers in which restraint of a coercive nature plays no part.

So, in summary, the one and only time I have ever commented on holding therapy was in a paragraph in a paper published in 2003, and that was it. End of.

All the best

David Howe

5th March 2012

David,

Remember that the paper was written jointly by Howe and S. I wrote mainly about the bits I knew about (mainly the first half of the paper) - the number of children adopted and in care, what happens developmentally to children who have suffered abuse, neglect etc before they came into care. S wrote about the therapeutic work done at K. So the division of labour was broadly me writing about the academic, theory and research background to what we know about children who come into care, and S writing about her practice. The two bits then got married together. As I wasn't a therapist, it was not my place to write about the therapy. But of course, because I am one of the named authors I can't disown the way the practice element of the paper was described - indeed, part of my reason for getting involved was to get a description of the treatment out into the public domain so that people could know what was involved, for good or ill.

As I said, my general belief that we should be open so that at least we all know what is going on is, looking back on it, probably naive but it was written in good faith - that is, to know is better than not to know otherwise people are liable to fantasise or invent. So whether the reader agreed with what was said or not, at least there was something concrete to react to and get at. And how!

Looking back of course, I can see that it would be reasonable to think that by helping to describe practice I was endorsing it, but I can't do much about that now. Of all the dozens of books and papers I have written over the last 30 odd years, the only time I've ever mentioned holding therapy is briefly in that one paper published in 2003. It just goes to show that you never know what's going to come back and bite you.

I don't know whether all my responses are helping or not, or what you would like to get out of them, but I'm trying to be as clear and honest as I can about the origins, background and creation of the paper, my involvement, and my very brief skirmish hearing about holding therapy.

All the best

David Howe

8th March 2012

David,

Sorry you're still confused. My only role was to agree, back in 2001, to help S. describe the work of the centre so that other people would at least know what they did rather than guess at what they did. In that sense, I naively thought I was doing everyone a favour by getting what was done out into the public domain so that people could at least either know what was going, criticise it, react to it in some way, etc. I wasn't (couldn't) endorse it as such because I'm not a therapist, I've never seen holding therapy, never practised at K. All I could do was help describe it so that other people could at least know what K was doing, whether they agreed with it or not. But of course, having agreed to help describe it, I became implicated, which was not very bright of me. As I say, given the hassle, I'm beginning to feel rather naive and regret that I ever became implicated, however indirectly or unwittingly. Hey ho.

Given what I know today, and given all the discussion, research evidence, arguments etc, my personal and current position continues to be that holding therapy is not appropriate and should play no part in helping, treating and supporting children in, or out of the care system. Modern evidence suggests much more appropriate and better ways of helping children based on attuned, sensitive, consistent, structured parenting.

I'm not sure how to make my position any clearer. I accept that ignorance is no excuse, but like you, where I was then and where I am now are very different places. We learn, we change, we move on.

I know that this is terribly important stuff for you and so I really don't mind you getting in touch.

Anyway, take care and continued very best wishes.

David Howe

Correspondence from Gregory Keck PhD to David Hanson

4th June 2012

The original work which included rage reduction therapy was first calle, I believe, the Z method-over 30 years ago maybe even over 35 years ago. Foster Cline,M.D. , revised that work and re-named it rage reduction/holding therapy. The theory was that lots of nurturing after confrontation and catharsis was critical for the healing process. So much has transpired in the field of trauma and attachment in the past 15-20 years in terms of what academicians and mental helath therapists have discovered. Neuroscience has afforded a great deal of information on which we base our work and interventions.

I'm not certain when most therapists began to transform their work, but I believe that were not doing the typical rage reduction work in the mid-late 1990s. Though, I do believe that it helped many people. In fact, I recently received two phone calls from people I saw 20 years ago indicating just how helpful therapy was for them. One of them, in fact, is himself working with adolescents in a juvenile correctional facility; he indicated that he was deeply grateful for the therapy we offered him. He was among the first people we treated and were doing the more intrusive confrontational therapy. He is in his 30s now and is quite happy.

I am sorry to hear that your experience was not a positive one. I have co-authored two books and did one alone. The first two, Adopting the Hurt Child (2009), Parenting the Hurt Child (2009), were revised and updated in 2009. They explain therapy and parenting techniques. The book I did alone, Parenting Adopted Adolescents(2009), discusses adolescence as a discreet developmental stage and how parents can help adopted adolescents mature and develop while addressing trauma and adoption related issues.

If you go to attach.org, there is a white paper there which discusses the current trend in attachment therapy. My books are available in the UK, though I do not know who the distributor is. Jessica Kingsley Publishers has a rather good selection of books related to therapy, attachment, and adoption.

I hope that you are able to find some answers to the questions you have. I have high regard for Dr. Howe's work.

Sincerely,

Greg

Gregory C. Keck,Ph.D.

5th June 2012

David,

I did training for Adopt UK-they sponsored it, and the training was for about 10-12 clinicians held in London. I do believe that I spoke at K and a couple of people came to the US to observe our work in my office. I did train the original group of therapists while Rage Reduction and Holding Therapy were being done in the US. I recall training Sa and one other person in the original group of people. I'm assuming that S trained her staff, though, I don't know.

I don't know why Dr. Howe apologized, but as I said earlier, we had very some very good outcomes. I don't think people stopped doing it becasue it was ineffective but rather that, in all professsions, there are new developments coming from new research. We are now doing eg neurofeedback which was not even developed when we began our work. If you could find a copy of Adopting the Hurt Child published in 1995 and updated in 1998, therapy was explicitly discussed as it was gong on then. In the 2005 edition, that chapter is completely updated. The initial book gives a thorough discussion of the theoretical framework for attachment therapy. Hopefully, very little that is current in mental health will be going on in 20 years. Dentstry, medicine, etc., evolve as new info is discovered, which is exactly what occurred in attachment therapy. It was always known that trauma caused attachment problems; today trauma is being discussed extensively in the mental health arena.

Greg

Correspondence from David Hughes PhD to David Hanson

13th June

Dear David,

In 1992 I went to the Attachment Center in Colorado and observed them doing holding therapy. I then incorporated some of the mild interventions that they did, including gentle and comforting holding of children by their parents or carers or therapist and therapeutic holding if a child was out of control. I never did the intrusive holding that I observed there, where they would provoke the child into anger. The mild interventions were incorporated in my early work which I wrote about in 1997 and 1998. Shortly after that I had eliminated all holding by therapists and found many ways to help children not go out of control so that the therapeutic holding was much less necessary. I also found ways to rely much less on consequences for managing children's assultive and challenging behavior. My books since then reflect those changes.

If there are still therapists doing holding therapy as you describe it, I believe that they are very secretive about it. They would probabl loose their license to practice as therapists if their professional boards found out that they were as, I believe, now all professionals would condemn that practice. I do not believe that there is any evidence that holding therapy is effective. I do not believe that why happened to you would be considered to be legal.

Best wishes

Dan Hughes

Correspondence from Dr Matt Woolgar to David Hanson

13th June 2012

Dear David

My colleague forwarded me your email to him as I have an active research and clinical interest in so called attachment therapies that are still, in some forms or other, perpetrated against looked after and adopted children. It is an interesting and helpful blog you are compiling, particularly as it is a UK perspective. More so now the kidscomefirst webpage doesn't seem to be around anymore, which is a shame as it was great resource, but of course it had a strong US component which let some of the UK clinicians I speak to say, 'Well it doesn't happen in the UK!' – but unfortunately it does. I have even seen a version practiced on a 10 year looked after child with autism who was waiting to be assessed by us at our National Adoption & Fostering Service. Both his 'attachment therapist' and his foster carer were pinning him down and forcing him to make eye contact, not because he was out of control and needed restraining but because they believed it to be 'therapeutic'. Their warped belief in its therapeutic power meant that they were happy to do this shocking and cruel 'treatment' in public. Clearly they knew nothing about autism and how aversive it can be for some children to make eye contact and I doubt it would happen to a birth child. But then I have seen a whole host of shocking treatments used against looked after and adopted children over the years. The worry for me is that there are new versions of holding around that are just as bizarre and unscientific but which minimise the explicit notion of holding, so they can slip underneath the radar but which still do things, in a similar vein, that are unproven, unhelpful and neglectful of what we know maltreated and neglected children need.

Again I doubt these unscientific and frankly bizarre approaches would be perpetrated against children living in their birth families – only against the vulnerable children separated from their families, and I wonder if that says something important about the people insisting upon these treatments. I often find myself thinking about why some therapists continue to use these approaches, even though the evidence is against them, especially if we assume they are (or have been at some point) committed to helping children. The best I can come up with is that people who have committed to training in this extreme way, with the hope of helping children, who have then bought into the philosophy of the programme and have been practicing it faithfully for years, still with hope and against all the accumulating evidence - then how hard must it be to turn around and say all those years of challenging sessions were dangerous nonsense? So perhaps their motivation derives from somewhere between cognitive dissonance and narcissism. Anyway I expect that whatever they say they do now, elements of it surreptitiously slip back in to what they practice even if they call it by a new name or keep it hidden – the therapist I saw pinning a child down identified as practitioner of a well-known brand of play therapy, even though such aversive practices would not be a core part of that model. Of course, there may also well be less charitable explanations for these practices continuing and I expect that your own experiences have caused you to think about that a lot. It is a shame. If former advocates could admit they had made mistakes, then I am sure it would do a lot of good for the current and future generations of maltreated and neglected children. Science progresses by acknowledging mistakes but the practitioners who hold these beliefs too often appear to be driven more by ideology than science.

117

The more people who know about the Chaffin et al (APSAC) 2006 and AACAP 2005 recommendations the better, so well done for citing them. I have given talks to groups of specialist clinicians working with looked after and adopted children and there have been large cohorts amongst them who have considered these sensible recommendations dangerous and assume that it is common knowledge that proven, well evidenced approaches do not apply to looked after and adopted children and that only the bizarre and extreme will work. Of course the evidence does not support such a negative approach and indeed the practice parameters recommend that we do thorough assessments, use the evidence base in any treatments, and avoid unproven holding or regression therapies. The dogged belief in bizarre treatments is an unscientific and dangerous ideology that continues to fail children and their carers, and I think these warped ideas come directly from holding therapy and the demonization of maltreated children that it implicitly promotes. Keep up the good work, making sure people hear your voice and your moving story, I shall certainly recommend your blog to others and will include a link to it in my future talks.

Best wishes

Matt

Dr Matt Woolgar

Clinical Psychologist & Project Lead, Evidence Based Measures of Parenting

National Academy for Parenting Research

King's College London

Acknowledgements

I owe debts to many people. First, I would like to express my gratitude to David Hanson. No one can doubt his courage and resilience. I would also like to thank Professor Jean Mercer for her support and for inspiring me through the elegance of her writing.

Then there were many others who, directly and indirectly, supported the campaign to raise awareness of Holding Therapy. These include Professor Edzard Ernst of the Peninsular Medical School; Dr Ben Goldacre of the *Guardian*; Professor David Howe; Dr Matt Woolgar of Kings College London; New-York-based journalist, Kathryn Joyce; Linda Rosa of Advocates for Children in Therapy; Clair Stoneman, partner in the law firm Foot Anstey and Rick Creswell at "The Company".

Made in the USA
Charleston, SC
21 August 2012